Ethnocentrism
in Its Many Guises

Ethnocentrism
in Its Many Guises

Edited by

Marjorie M. Snipes

Selected Papers from the Annual Meeting of the
Southern Anthropological Society,
Carrollton, Georgia,
March 23–25, 2017

Betty J. Duggan
SAS Proceedings Interim Series Editor

Newfound Press
THE UNIVERSITY OF TENNESSEE LIBRARIES, KNOXVILLE

Southern Anthropological Society
Founded 1966

Ethnocentrism in Its Many Guises
© 2021 by Southern Anthropological Society: *southernanthro.org*

Print on demand available through University of Tennessee Press.
DOI: https://doi.org/10.7290/c8d93j5

For all other uses, contact:
Newfound Press
University of Tennessee Libraries
1015 Volunteer Boulevard
Knoxville, TN 37996-1000
newfoundpress.utk.edu

ISBN-13: 978-1-953291-00-4 (paperback)
ISBN-13: 978-1-953291-01-1 (PDF)

Names: Snipes, Marjorie M., author, editor. | Southern Anthropological Society. Meeting
    (2017: Carrollton, Ga.)
Title: Ethnocentrism in its many guises / edited by Marjorie M. Snipes.
Description: Knoxville, Tennessee : Newfound Press, University of Tennessee Libraries,
    [2021] | 1 online resource : color illustrations | Series: Southern Anthropological
    Society proceedings ; no. 46 | General Note: "Selected Papers from the Annual
    Meeting of the Southern Anthropological Society, Carrollton, Georgia, March 23–25,
    2017." | Includes bibliographical references.
Identifiers: ISBN-13: 9781953291011 (PDF) | ISBN-13: 9781953291004 (paperback)
Subjects: LCSH: Immigrants—Mexican-American Border Region—Social conditions—
    Congresses. | Border crossing—Mexican-American Border Region—Congresses.
    | Indigenous peoples—Abuse of—Canada—Congresses. | Reconciliation—Social
    aspects—Canada—Congresses. | Mandjak (African people)—Cabo Verde—Social
    conditions—Congresses. | Foreign workers, African—Cabo Verde—Social conditions
    —Congresses. | Nutrition—Study and teaching—North Carolina—Congresses. |
    Refugees—Nutrition—North Carolina—Congresses. | Wu-Tang Clan (Musical group)
    —Criticism and interpretation—Congresses. | Rap (Music)—History and criticism—
    Congresses. | African Americans—Music—History and criticism—Congresses. |
    Ethnocentrism—Congresses. | Ethnology—Congresses.
Classification: LCC GN495.8 .E85 2021eb (PDF) | LCC GN495.8 .E85 2021 (print)

Book design by Martha Rudolph
Cover design by C. S. Jenkins

Contents

CHAPTER 1

The Many Guises of Ethnocentrism

Marjorie M. Snipes

Prelude

The planning phase for the 2017 Annual Meetings of the Southern Anthropological Society in Carrollton, Georgia, began shortly after the 2016 elections, which represented a significant shift in politics and social life in the United States. The new President, with an "America First" agenda focusing quite entirely on one cultural vision and one cultural definition using criteria that surprised the majority of people, heralded the meaning, significance, and dangers of ethnocentrism in ways that shook and disrupted the citizenry. Even as early as December 2016, it seemed urgent that we, as anthropologists, reexamine foundational concepts like ethnocentrism, cultural relativism, and racism in deeper and more provocative ways than we had grown accustomed to. The spirit and earlier works of our disciplinary fore-parents, such as Franz Boas, Melville Herskovits, W. E. B. DuBois, and Zora Neale Hurston, called out to be reexamined and remembered—tied back into our central goals as social scientists now in the twenty-first century. And, so, the conference theme, "Ethnocentrism," made itself felt all around us as we watched citizenry protest through marches, letter-writing campaigns to politicians, media posts, bumper stickers, and ongoing yard signs.

The election had initiated us into a period of liminality where we were not sure where we were heading and most of us, regardless of our positionality, remained anxious and without clear expectations. Emotions were raw, and the sense of common trust and fraternity that many of us had known prior to the election ended rather abruptly. As we grappled to understand what was happening and sought a foothold to allow us to respond, many of us, as social scientists, began looking for historical patterns. This conference was to be a forum in which we could examine all types of ethnocentrism and ways that communities could respond. We considered many angles of ethnocentrism, including nationalism and partisanship, looking to other countries, other cultures, and other times in an attempt to better grasp what was happening all around us.

Word and Concept

The concept of ethnocentrism has roots deep in our anthropological heritage. Although many social scientists attribute its coinage to William Graham Sumner in his 1906 book, *Folkways*, Bizumic (2014, 7), building on earlier research of Bracq (1902) and Banton (1998), traces the concept of ethnocentrism to the writings of Ludwig Gumplowicz (ca. 1879). Because Gumplowicz's work, published significantly earlier than Sumner's, was available only in German and Polish, it appears that Sumner "leaned" on the concept and identified it in 1906 to a wide group of English-speaking social scientists with no reference to the earlier scholar. Sumner did further develop the idea and provided us with a perspective that is most commonly in use today.

This early work already foretold the complexity and hydra-like quality of ethnocentrism. Gumplowicz ([1899], 155-6) used the term *syngenism* to refer to the feeling, the attraction that individuals have for a unity of sameness:

> Man is not so bad as crass materialism pictures him; neither is he so large hearted as Christian philosophy in

vain requires him to be. He is neither devil nor angel, simply human. Fettered to the community by natural ties of blood, habit and mood of thought, his egoism is social, his sympathies are social; to demand more than social sympathy is to demand something unnatural and superhuman and to credit him with less than social egoism is to do him wrong. But social egoism includes social sympathy, social sympathy is social egoism. Let us call their union syngenism and we have identified the motive of all social development and the key to its solution.

Developing further this idea of in-group/out-group, Sumner writes ([1906] 2008, 15):

Ethnocentrism is . . . this view of things in which one's own group is the center of everything, and all others are scaled and rated with reference to it. . . . Each group nourishes its own pride and vanity, boasts itself superior, exalts its own divinities, and looks with contempt on outsiders. Each group thinks its own folkways the only right ones, and if it observes that other groups have other folkways, these excite its scorn. Opprobrious epithets are derived from these differences. "Pig-eater," "cow-eater," "uncircumcised," "jabberers," are epithets of contempt and abomination. . . . For our present purpose the most important fact is that ethnocentrism leads a people to exaggerate and intensify everything in their own folkways which is peculiar and which differentiates them from others.

And what constitutes the group? Interestingly, although ethnocentrism is a concept that decidedly carries the idea that there is an openly-acknowledged shared ethnicity among a group of people, Sumner effortlessly translates this concept to the state and a sense of nationhood *as if it were its own ethnicity* (ibid., 19):

3

> All states give the same security and conditions of welfare to all. The standards of civic institutions are the same, or tend to become such, and it is a matter of pride in each state to offer civic status and opportunities equal to the best. Every group of any kind whatsoever demands that each of its members shall help defend group interests. Every group stigmatizes anyone who fails in zeal, labor, and sacrifices for group interests. Thus the sentiment of loyalty to the group, or the group head, which was so strong in the Middle Ages, is kept up, as far as possible, in regard to modern states and governments. The group force is also employed to enforce the obligations of devotion to group interests. It follows that judgments are precluded and criticism is silenced.

Yet, unlike nationalism, ethnocentrism carries with it a sense of kinship (Milhayi 1985, 106). This fictive biological foundation makes the group seem natural and effortless. Where individuals otherwise might seek to distinguish themselves from a unified group, under conditions of ethnocentrism these same individuals will sense a pull towards a larger, more cohesive identity. Émile Durkheim, sensing this same divide between the individual and the group identity, referred to this as a double being: "an individual being which has its foundation in the organism and whose activities are therefore strictly limited, and a social being which represents the highest reality on the intellectual and moral order that we can know by observation—I mean society" (cited in Leaf 1979, 163). Who we are depends on both self and group—and humans as individuals are members of many different groups. It is our social natures, the give and take of identities, that define us.

Interestingly, both scholars, Gumplowicz and Sumner, noted that ethnocentrism also frequently pairs itself with religion, providing a legitimacy and basis to claim moral rectitude (Bizumic 2014, 5).

A Dangerous Hydra

Ethnocentrism can be imagined as a capricious hydra. Group identity, critical as a cohesive and active force, provides individuals with assets and advantages. It allows for enhanced security and protection, for the ability to alter and manipulate social and physical environments, and for leverage in a wide range of activities. While humans have always used kinship as a grouping mechanism, with the development of ethnocentrism these same humans could now belong to non-kin groupings and motivate others to align with any number of causes and interests. Ethnocentrism is effective. It works well at keeping individuals together, in line, affirmed.

It also is the groundwork for cultural diversity. When separate groups form, they distinguish themselves along certain well-worn paths best exemplified through Durkheim's definition of religion. While he referred to these as differences of religion, they also adhere to the distinctions between any kinds of groups, sacred or secular: differences in ritual, belief, forms of organization, and ethic norms (values) (Durkheim 1995, 44). It is ethnocentrism which allows for the development of difference within the group—the idea that one practice or belief is better than another, more commonsensical, more just, more efficient. And from *so simple a beginning*[1] ... have emerged all sorts of hydra-like consequences: from pride, dignity and distinction, to competition, discrimination, warfare, genocide. Like so many critical concepts, ethnocentrism, too, is a cline. It contributes significantly to our ability to survive in a mild form by prompting differences that allow for cross-fertilizations, re-imaginings, competitive drives, and innovations, yet in its most destructive form it leads humans to seek the extermination of those who are different. How to control this "beastly" force has grown to have the most significant impacts since the development of state societies.

Causes and Relief

In this little volume, we seek to provide our readers with examples of ethnocentrism in its various guises across time, genres, and cultures. Our authors, using their various specialties within anthropology, have considered the form and impact of ethnocentrism in multiple areas—from historic treaties between nations and ways of defining selfhood as a nation within a state society to ethnocentric applications within music and health. Seeing the creative diversity and intensity of ethnocentrism reminds us that even today, as we face increasingly visible signs of social fracture within nation-states, we are dealing with a well-worn friend and foe.

In Chapter 2, "Borders and Bridges," Christine Kovic's cogent scholarship on the "policies of exclusion" draws our attention to ethnocentrism in policy and practice around us, right now, being perpetrated in our names at the international border between the United States and Mexico. Her work calls us to respond urgently to these violations of human rights that are causing suffering and death. These lines being drawn between Us and Them reverberate and percolate all throughout our society—as she says, "policies also cross borders." She urges us to connect the dots between what is happening on the border and perspectives and actions occurring within all levels of our society. Whether you live along the border or deep within the "heartland," our country (and other countries) are immediately impacted by ethnocentric policies.

Chapter 3, "Examination of the Reconciliation Movement in the Canadian Cultural Genocide," draws our attention across the northern border and into Canada, focusing on the history, challenges, and failures within the Canadian reconciliation movement with Aboriginal peoples. Yeju Choi deftly documents the historical roots of this process, reminding us of the context of reconciliation amidst cultural genocide and deceit. Although Canada established the Truth and Reconciliation Commission in 2006 and tried to utilize methods such as storytelling to encourage open dialogues about past abuses and possible ways to mend the social fabric between immigrant-citizens and first peoples, this process was flawed. Choi reminds us that when those in power determine the methods and means of reconciliation, it perpetrates abuse, regardless of the stated goals and objectives. A process that appeared to seek healing "strengthened the stereotypes and biases against Aboriginal people."

Brandon Lundy and Kezia Darkwah examine the immigrant Manjaco peoples of Cabo Verde (Cape Verde) in Chapter 4, "Becoming Manjaco." Serving as a buffer of sorts between Africa and Europe, Cabo Verde is today a vibrant and tense melting pot of diverse cultures and ethnicities. From their work in ethnographic surveys of Bissau-Guinean immigrants on the islands of Boa Vista and Santiago, Lundy and Darkwah direct our attention to the politics of *othering* via economic disparity and geographical longevity among immigrant groups. Their work, while pointing out the discrimination and violation of immigrant rights in Cabo Verde, also suggests that effective and culturally sensitive immigration policies do have "a clear effect on both local receptivity and foreign guests' community integration." While ethnocentrism challenges nation-states, it can be managed better when federal policies align with humanitarian principles, resulting in a more unified and stable society.

In Chapter 5, "Through a Glass Darkly," Kathleen and Daniel Ingersoll take a broader perspective on ethnocentrism, looking at how other cultures and other historical periods are framed and depicted from the lens of the observers. Using the example of Rapa Nui where they have done anthropological research for more than a decade, the Ingersolls trace the depiction and appreciation for the monumental architecture on Rapa Nui as a function of our own ethnocentric cultural biases in which we aggrandize the monumental and project our own cultural values onto what we encounter, remaining oblivious to the potential of finding new ways to understand. It is a cultivated ignorance.

Ethnocentrism extends beyond cultures; it also projects distinctions within a same culture and impacts sub-cultural groups in various ways. In Chapter 6, "Feeding Variety," Ayla Samli looks at the ethnocentrism of nutritional access and standards in the American diet as it affects schoolchildren and adult refugees. Her work reminds us of the socioeconomics of food, which intersects with identity and health and is deeply ethnocentric. Samli argues that the standards of nutrition used in social institutions throughout the United States are themselves based more on identities and the intersections between economics, politics, and history than on biology and nutritional needs. Her research, though, ends on a positive note about ethnocentrism: she imagines "nutrition classes where newly arrived refugees and immigrants participate alongside of their Title 1 counterparts to explore, sample, and enjoy exciting and healthy flavors and possibilities from an array of cultural backgrounds." In short, she pushes us to see ethnocentrism as a culinary delight that results in healthier people biologically and socially.

Our final chapter, Chapter 7, "The Wu Tang Clan and Cultural Resistance," pushes us to consider the language and symbolism of ethnocentrism in the genre of music, actually inviting us to consider this from multiple perspectives. In a detailed and sensitive analysis of the Wu Tang playlist and its musical roots, Michael Blum examines the ways that ethnocentrism has been called out by those suffering its effects. Not only do we hear the drama of ethnocentrism in the lyrics of Wu Tang, but we also experience it as readers. Listening to these words—many sharp-edged and socially astute—calling out conditions that have oppressed peoples over long periods and been too invisible for too long, Blum's fearless hand keeps us moving along the trajectory of this extraordinary musical group's documentation of society-as-it-is for too many today.

Notes

1. These are the words that Charles Darwin used to refer to the origin of species from a single-celled organism.

Bibliography

Banton, M. 1998. *Racial Theories*. 2nd ed. Cambridge: Cambridge University Press.

Bizumic, Boris. 2014. "Who Coined the Concept of Ethnocentrism? A Brief Report." *Journal of Social and Political Psychology* 2 (1): 3–10.

Bracq, J. C. 1902. "A Stronger Sense of International Justice Needed." In *Report of the Eighth Annual Lake Mohonk Conference on International Arbitration*, edited by William J. Rose, 18–22. Mohonk Lake, NY: Lake Mohonk Arbitration Conference.

Durkheim, Émile. (1912) 1995. *The Elementary Forms of the Religious Life*. Translated by Karen Fields. New York: Free Press.

Gumplowicz, Ludwig. *The Outlines of Sociology*. Translated by Frederick W. Moore. Philadelphia: American Academy of Political and Social Science, 1899; Internet Archive, 2017. https://archive.org/details/in.ernet. dli.2015.201716/page/n9.

Hammond, Ross A. and Robert Axelrod. 2006. "The Evolution of Ethnocentrism." *Journal of Conflict Resolution* 50 (6): 926–936.

Leaf, Murray J. 1979. *Man, Mind, and Science*. New York: Columbia University Press.

Milhayi, Louis J. 1985. "Ethnocentrism vs. Nationalism: Origin and Fundamental Aspects of a Major Problem for the Future." *Humboldt Journal of Social Relations* 12 (1): 95–113. Fall/Winter 1984–85.

Sumner, William Graham. *Folkways: A Study of the Sociological Importance of Usages, Manners, Customs, Mores, and Morals*. Boston: Ginn, 1906; Project Gutenberg, 2008. Mark C. Orton, Turgut Dincer, et al., text preparers. https://www.gutenberg.org/files/24253/24253-h/24253-h.htm.

CHAPTER 2

Borders and Bridges: Migration, Anthropology, and Human Rights

Christine Kovic

> *"Los sueños también viajan. . . ."*
> ("Dreams also travel. . . .")
> Mural in Soup Kitchen in
> La Patrona, Veracruz, Mexico

"Ethnocentrism and Its Many Guises," the theme of the Southern Anthropological Society's March 2017 conference, emerged from the urgency of the contemporary social and political context. Marjorie Snipes's poetic and powerful introduction to the conference program affirmed that anthropologists and students of anthropology have an ethical responsibility to stand up for diversity, stand against discrimination, stand with those at risk and suffering threats, and stand out in support of ethical research. The conference took place just two months after the inauguration of Donald Trump, a president who ran on a campaign to build a physical wall at the US–Mexico border, and whose words and actions were openly xenophobic, racist, Islamophobic, and sexist, constantly playing on people's fear of "others." At his inauguration, he promised "From this day forward, it's going to be only America First," an ethnocentric platform tied to the extraction of wealth from and great violence to other nations. While the United Nations decried one of the largest numbers of displaced people and refugees in the world, President Trump lowered the cap of refugees admitted to the United States and excluded refugees from seven Muslim-majority countries.

Yet much of what is taking place under the current administration is not new. Rather, current policies only build on deep-rooted racism, xenophobia, and class inequalities that have been in place for years. As stated in the title of Paul Kramer's op-ed in the *New York Times*, "Trump's Anti-Immigrant Racism Represents an American Tradition." Take, for instance, Trump's promise to build "a great wall" between the United States and Mexico. For two decades, the US has intensified enforcement and militarization at its southern border, not to mention the 700 miles of border fencing that already exist. Upwards of 7,000 migrants have perished in attempts to cross the border or the southern US in dangerous conditions—deaths resulting directly from immigration and enforcement policies. Anthropologists challenge ethnocentrism because it entails much more than offensive words; it is the policies of exclusion that cause suffering and even death. In the case of current immigration and border policy in the United States, some lives are valued more than others, leaving working poor migrants, especially people of color, at risk of injury, assault, or death as they attempt to cross international borders.

This brief essay, drawn from my keynote address at the 2017 conference, focuses on anthropology as a tool for studying borders and bridges. Borders are at once physical boundaries within and between nations and less visible policies that create and sustain inequalities.[1] I point to some of the ways that anthropology can be useful in documenting the exclusion and racism of border policies through two case studies. The first is that of Central Americans attempting to cross Mexico *en route* to the United States, and the second is of Mexican and Central American migrants who perish in attempts to cross South Texas. Both cases illustrate the ways borders—physical and ideological—cause violence to those who are not defined as legitimate members of the nation. At the same time, migrants themselves, activists, and organizations create multiple bridges across difference in attempts to challenge racism and support immigrant rights. As stated in the epigraph, migrants travel because they dream, and they seek to build lives free of violence.

I was attracted to Anthropology because of its potential to locate the ways policies, regardless of intention, can contribute to suffering. My training as a graduate student at City University of New York (CUNY) prepared me to challenge ethnocentrism and, in particular, to document and challenge exploitation in its multiple forms. When I began graduate school in 1990, I was most fortunate to be surrounded by a group of students and faculty who sought through anthropology to uncover "relationships of power and structures of inequality," in the words of Leith Mullings, one my first professors in graduate school (2015, 5). We grappled with anthropology's colonial history and sought out some of the early critiques of this perspective, reading Kathleen Gough, Dell Hymes, Rodolfo Stavenhagen, and Faye Harrison. In a graduate school located in mid-town Manhattan, we constantly connected what we were reading and discussing in the classroom to current events. We protested the US invasion of Iraq in 1991 (later named the First Gulf War), marched in the streets in 1992 demonstrating against the acquittal of officers who had been recorded on videotape beating Rodney King. This was also a time of budget cuts to higher education, with Governor Mario Cuomo proposing cutting the budget of all schools of the City University of New York by ten percent and raising tuition to help pay for the cuts. This sparked a student strike at the CUNY campuses, and the students at the Graduate Center "occupied" the building for ten days in 1991, demanding support for public higher education (McCaffrey, Kovic, and Menzies 2020). All of these events influenced my own relationships to anthropology and my research projects. To quote

Leith Mullings, we saw that the circumstances surrounding us, "war, violence, racism, and poverty, were not 'natural' or given" but "created in a specific political and historic context" (2015, 5).

My own research over the past decade has centered on borders and border crossers, including the human rights of Central American and Mexican migrants at the Texas–Mexico border, in south Texas, and at Mexico's "vertical border," which extends from its southern border with Guatemala to the Rio Grande. The US concept of Homeland Security justifies the protection of certain groups of American citizens while excluding anyone defined as being outside the "homeland." Contemporary security policies are part and parcel of American imperialism—that is, US law has a long history of making distinctions between insiders and outsiders, between those who are deserving of citizenship rights and those who may provide profit through low-paid work precisely because they are viewed as "deportable" and "disposable." US immigration law is based on exclusion, with historic examples of the Chinese Exclusion Act of 1882 and the Oriental Exclusion Act of 1924. The Johnson–Reed Immigration Act of 1924 favored certain groups of immigrants as it limited entry of southern and eastern Europeans and large categories of Asians who were deemed undesirable (Molina 2014). Under President Eisenhower, the United States deported more than one million people from the US Southwest to Mexico—some of whom were US citizens—in a 1954 immigration enforcement policy named "Operation Wetback," a racial slur (Ngai 2014). The 1995 Border Patrol initiative in San Diego, California, "Operation Gatekeeper," increased enforcement near the urban area, pushing migrants to cross in isolated and dangerous conditions. The title "Gatekeeper" evokes the distinctions made at the border between those who are valued and those who are not allowed to enter.

In the contemporary period, large categories of working poor migrants are largely excluded from entering the United States through legal channels. Central Americans (principally from Honduras, El Salvador, and Guatemala) and Mexicans without large bank accounts are largely unable to obtain a visa to legally cross Mexico or to enter the US. These migrants cross Mexico in a dangerous journey in which they risk assault, rape, dismemberment, and death. They cross Mexico's southern and northern borders as well as the entire Mexican nation, a territory that has become a vertical border where they encounter violence at the hands of police, military, migration officials, narco-traffickers, and common criminals. In broad terms, security is defined as freedom from risk and danger; however, recent security policies created in the United States and Mexico produce the risk, danger, and human rights abuses that Central American migrants encounter. Instead of being protected by state agents and security policies, migrants become targets of these forces and are met with violence on their journey.

Migrants who cannot afford to pay *coyotes* (guides) to help them cross Mexico, ride atop the freight train, popularly known as *la bestia* (the beast) and now popularized in films such as *La Jaula de Oro: The Golden Dream*; *Sin Nombre*; *Which Way Home*; and Pedro Ultrera's *La Bestia*. The freight train provides a metaphor for global capitalism. The cargo moves inside cars, protected from the elements and sometimes with private security guards, while migrants ride atop the train, vulnerable to weather, power lines, and falling to the tracks. The working poor cross borders in dangerous conditions, while commodities and capital cross freely. Many Central Americans suffer injury or death on their journey through Mexico. These are not accidents but policy outcomes. To give but one example, in Apizaco, in the state of Tlaxcala in central Mexico, a series of concrete posts have been built surrounding the train tracks near a station. When migrants are injured by the posts as they jump from the train—posts deliberately placed—their injuries are not accidents.

Not everyone who crosses Mexico faces the violence of security. Those defined as marginal—those who "look" poor or Central American—are most likely to be stopped by security agents or targeted by organized criminals. This reveals one of the many ways borders create and reinforce inequalities. In Trinitaria, Mexico, the government built a huge security checkpoint in 2015, located just miles from the border with Guatemala. The Trinitaria "super checkpoint" is one of five planned for the southern border region. Every car, bus, motorcycle, and even bicycle must pass through an entire security complex named "Center for Comprehensive Care for Border Transit" (*Centro de Atención Integral al Tránsito Fronteriza* in Spanish). Migrants without visas attempt to avoid these checkpoints, traveling in clandestine conditions and increasing their vulnerability to assault. As a white woman, I pass through every time without revision, no request for a passport, not even a question. Security agents determine who can cross and who will be detained, a determination based on race and class. Indeed, indigenous Mexicans, particularly Mayans from Chiapas, have been detained in northern Mexico and "accused" of being in the country without permission (Lakhani 2016). These cases point both to the ways that racial profiling targets those with darker skin and the marginality of indigenous peoples within Mexico.

Policies also cross borders. Connecting the dots shows the close, but profoundly unequal, relationship between the United States, Mexico, and Central America and the ways US policies lead to the violence of security. So-called free trade policies, such as the North American Free Trade Agreement (NAFTA), displaced small-scale rural producers due to the cheap and highly subsidized corn from the US that flooded Mexico. US support of repressive regimes in Central America, including the military governments of El Salvador and Guatemala during the civil wars of the 1960s–1990s, in which tens of thousands were killed, leaves a long legacy of militarization and violence. In more recent times, the US government, through political pressure and funding, has pushed Mexico to close its southern border to Central Americans. Mexico's narrowest point, the Isthmus of Tehuantepec, just 120 miles at its narrowest point, is much smaller than the US–Mexico border, which spans close to 2,000 miles. In 2015, Mexico deported a record number of Central Americans, and, in 2016, it deported more than the United States, making it appear that the US is outsourcing border enforcement.

Activists and migrants are able to connect the dots of US policies to the violence of security. To give one story from a shelter in southern Mexico: In July 2010, when I was at the shelter Home of Mercy in Arriaga, Chiapas, news arrived that the freight train was preparing to leave, and everyone who was staying rushed to the railroad tracks about a mile away to stake out a place for themselves. When I later walked to the train myself and found the migrants waiting for it to depart, several were eager to talk to me. One man explained why he had left his home country, Honduras, and was now beginning his journey North. He asked if I had heard of the Central American Free Trade Agreement (CAFTA) and explained that his family made shoes. With CAFTA, they could no longer compete with cheap imports, and now he was forced to search for work in the North. He presented a concise critique of "free trade" and also contested the label of criminal, insisting that leaving his country to look for work should not be considered a crime. After explaining the reasons he was going North, he paused, smiled, and said, "It's ok, one day my son will be president of the United States." Perhaps he was joking, yet his comment was an insistence on inclusion with full rights. If migrants see the powerful links between free trade agreements and the displacement of the working poor, those with power and privilege must also make these links. In short, the construction of "illegality" through borders serves as an unrecognized glue that legitimates exploitation.

The violence of security extends to the US–Mexico border and the southern United States. According to official US Border Patrol records, over 7,000 border crossers have perished along the US–Mexico border between 1998 and 2017. This averages more than one death per day. Hundreds die each year from heat exhaustion, drowning in the Rio Grande, car crashes, and other causes. In Texas, the state where I live, migrants die as they cross the US–Mexico border, and they also die in South Texas. In 2012, migrant deaths in Texas surpassed those in the state of Arizona; and, in 2014, deaths in the Rio Grande Valley sector (a region made up of 34 counties as defined by the US Border Patrol) surpassed those for the state of Arizona. Following scholars and activists who point to the structures behind these deaths, I label this violence "death by policy" to underscore the role of US immigration law, intensified enforcement, and neoliberal economic policies in causing these deaths.[2] Raquel Rubio Goldsmith uses the term "funnel effect" to describe the way increased enforcement channels migrants to dangerous areas where they may suffer injury and death.

This death count is far from complete, as it does not include those recovered on the Mexico side of the border and the many remains that are never recovered in the desert of Arizona and brush of South Texas. In Brooks County, just a four-hour drive from my home in Houston, hundreds of migrants have died in the past five years as they attempted to circumvent a border patrol checkpoint located 70 miles north of the border. This checkpoint and a parallel checkpoint in Sarita (Kenedy County) create what functions as a second border for anyone who appears "foreign." At these two checkpoints, one on Highway 281 and another on Highway 77, all northbound vehicles are stopped. Those who look like they do not belong are asked for documents. As a white woman, I never have been asked for any identification, and, most often, I am simply waived through the checkpoint.

Adding to the complexity and tragedy of the loss of life, local and state officials were not carrying out DNA testing—as required by Texas State Law for unidentified remains—in a standardized and coordinated manner to identify the dead. As such, migrants are "the new disappeared," to use a term from the 1970s and 1980s to name those who disappeared in the Civil Wars and repressive military regimes in Central and South America.[3] In June 2014, a group of anthropology students from the University of Indianapolis and Baylor University conducted an exhumation in Sacred Heart Cemetery in Brooks County, Texas. The cemetery is the site of burials of many of the Mexican and Central American migrants who died crossing South Texas, particularly the John and Jane Does or the unidentified migrants who cannot be returned to their families. The forensic anthropologists located 118 sets of human remains, buried haphazardly, without clear records, in biohazard trash bags, grocery bags, milk crates, or wrapped in cloth. A green plastic bag with one set of remains read "Dignity," a reference to a funeral brand of the Houston-based Service Corporation. The news of the burials made front-page headlines in the US and elsewhere, with Mark Colette's *Corpus Christi Caller Times* article titled "Mass Graves of Migrants Found in Falfurrias, Texas." Although the media attention focused on the way the remains were buried, the scandal behind this is the lack of coordinated efforts to identify the dead when they are presumed to be border crossers in South Texas. Yet the burning issue more commonly ignored is the fact that border deaths happen in any case. Why should people die? Why do some die as they seek work, join their families, or flee violence in their home countries? Why are those with wealth able to travel freely, while those without must travel at great risk?

Countless acts of bridging, of solidary with migrants, exist in Mexico, at the border, and in the United States. A network of shelters throughout Mexico and along the border, the vast majority connected to the Catholic Church, provide a relatively safe space for migrants to rest, share a meal, spend the night, and seek medical attention. Shelters, as well as human rights organizations, document abuses against migrants and challenge state officials who are responsible. Family members and migrants themselves organize searches for their loved ones and work to promote migrant rights. One story of a woman in South Texas illustrates the relentless persistence of families in seeking those who have disappeared. In 2014, a Guatemalan woman was traveling with other migrants through the South Texas brush in Brooks County when a Honduran woman in the group fell ill. The group was going to leave her behind, as is a common practice with guides, but the Guatemalan woman stayed with the Honduran and called for help. No one came and the woman's condition worsened. The Guatemalan woman went to seek assistance and got lost in the brush. Eventually, she found the highway, where she was picked up by Border Patrol. She begged them to search for the Honduran woman who had been left behind, but they refused. In just days, the Guatemalan woman was deported back to Guatemala. If she had not waited with the second woman, she likely would have reached her family in Virginia. From Guatemala, she kept calling the South Texas Human Rights Center in Falfurrias, Texas, sending a hand-drawn map to try to help locate the woman. Initially, her hope was that the woman was alive, but in time, she hoped her remains could be recovered for her family. While some might view her as courageous or a good Samaritan, in the US she is defined as an illegal, a criminal.

Anthropologists have played an important role in writing rights, that is, in documenting human rights abuses in the United States and globally—but also in documenting the ways people organize to resist abuses and to promote human rights broadly. Anthropologists are able to connect the dots, that is, to trace concrete polices behind abuses, from so-called "security" policies, to immigration policies, and economic policies. In listening to the stories of migrants, anthropologists do not have talking points and narrow approaches to changes. Instead, anthropologists place stories within a broader political and economic context, documenting the ways borders produce and re-inforce inequalities, as well as the ways solidarity attempts to build bridges across differences.

Notes

1. Gloria Anzaldúa's *Borderlands/La Frontera* conceptualizes the border as both a geographic space and a concept to understand identity and inequality.
2. Maria Jiménez (2009) uses the term "death by policy" to describe border deaths, drawing on the work of anthropologist Maurizio Albahari (2006).
3. Lynn Stephen (2008) writes of the "new disappeared, assassinated, and dead" to describe those who have met violence on the US–Mexico border in the contemporary period.

Bibliography

Albahari, Mauricio. 2006. *Death and the Modern State: Making Borders and Sovereignty at the Southern Edges of Europe.* San Diego: Center for Comparative Immigration Studies, University of California.

Álvarez, Robert R. Jr. 1995. "The Mexican–U.S. Border: The Making of an Anthropology of Borderlands." *Annual Review of Anthropology* 24: 447–470.

Anzaldúa, Gloria. 1987. *Borderlands: La Frontera.* San Francisco: Aunt Lute Books.

Jiménez, Maria. 2009. *Humanitarian Crisis: Migrant Deaths at the U.S.–Mexico Border.* San Diego and Mexico City: American Civil Liberties Union of San Diego and Imperial Counties and Mexico's National Commission of Human Rights.

Kramer, Paul. "Trump's Anti-Immigrant Racism Represents an American Tradition." *New York Times*, January 22, 2018.

Lakhani, Nina. "Mexico Tortures Migrants—and Citizens—in Effort to Slow Central American Surge." *The Guardian,* April 4, 2016.

McCaffrey, Katherine, Christine Kovic, and Charles Menzies. 2020. "On Strike: Student Activism, CUNY, and Engaged Anthropology." *Transforming Anthropology* 28 (2): 169–182.

Molina, Natalia. 2014. *How Race is Made in America: Immigration, Citizenship, and the Historical Power of Racial Scripts.* Berkeley: University of California Press.

Mullings, Leith. 2015. "Anthropology Matters, Presidential Address." *American Anthropologist* 17 (1): 4–16.

Ngai, Mae M. 2014. *Impossible Subjects: Illegal Aliens and the Making of Modern America.* Princeton: Princeton University Press.

Stephen, Lynn. 2008. "*Los Nuevos Desaparecidos y Muertos:* Immigration, Militarization, Death and Disappearance on Mexico's Borders." In *Security Disarmed: Critical Perspectives on Gender, Race, and Militarization*, edited by Barbara Sutton, Sandra Morgen, and Julie Novkov, 79–100. New Brunswick, NJ: Rutgers University Press.

CHAPTER 3

Examination of the Reconciliation Movement in the Canadian Cultural Genocide

Yeju Choi

Introduction and Literature Review

From the mid-1880s to the 1980s, the Canadian government established a partnership with churches and aimed to "'civilize' and Christianize, and ultimately, assimilate Aboriginal people into the Canadian society" (Truth and Reconciliation Commission of Canada 2008, 2). They forcibly separated Aboriginal children aged five to sixteen from their families and forced them to attend residential schools with the intent to destroy Aboriginal culture (MacDonald and Hudson 2012, 431). In 1920, the Deputy Minister of Indian Affairs even argued that their goal was to get rid of Aboriginal culture in Canada by assimilating all of them (Miller 2004, 35).

For that reason, residential schools did not allow indigenous parents to contact their children. The children were punished for speaking Aboriginal languages. Also, since there was no policy for discipline in these schools, the discipline was harsh (Miller 2004, 183). Verbal and physical abuse were very common in these residential schools, and sexual abuse was not uncommon. Since schools were hastily and cheaply built, diet and medical care were so poor for these children that many children also died from being sick (TRC 2008, 4). Furthermore, these schools did not inform parents even when their children died or ran away from school. Therefore, a significant number of Aboriginal children who attended residential schools are still missing, and many survivors are still suffering psychologically or physically (Royal Commission on Aboriginal Peoples 1996).

The definition of genocide by the United Nations (1948) includes "acts committed with intent to destroy, in whole or in part, a national, ethnical, racial or religious group . . . by forcibly transferring children of the group to another group" (United Nations 1948, 280). Therefore, many Aboriginal leaders and scholars refer to the Indian Residential School (IRS) system as cultural genocide conducted by the Canadian federal government (Akhtar 2010; MacDonald and Hudson 2012; Woolford 2009).

Residential schools were closed in the 1980s, and the information about these residential schools was known to the public from the 1990s. Consequently, the churches that ran residential schools started apologizing for their attempt at cultural genocide of Aboriginal people. The Canadian government established the Truth and Reconciliation Commission (TRC) and compensated all residential school survivors through the Indian Residential Settlement Agreement in 2006. Also, the Canadian government officially made an apology to Aboriginal people in 2008. In this recent reconciliation movement, the TRC set as their aim "to lay a foundation for the . . . reconciliation" (TRC 2015, vi). And the definition of reconciliation used by the TRC was the "establish[ment] and maint[enance] of respectful relationships" between Aboriginal people and non-Aboriginal people in Canada (TRC 2015, 16).

To achieve this goal of reconciliation, the TRC used storytelling (TRC 2015). In their report, the TRC gave the reasons for using storytelling as their reconciliation method: "It restores the human dignity of victims of violence and calls governments and citizens to account. Without truth, justice is not served, healing cannot happen, and there can be no genuine reconciliation between Aboriginal and non-Aboriginal peoples in Canada" (TRC 2015, 12). They claimed that storytelling could contribute to finding the truth because it gives voices to the survivors. Furthermore, they contended that once the truth was revealed, restorative justice could take place, which could bring healing for the victims and reconciliation of the society.

This argument of the TRC was reasonable, since many scholars have advocated for the role of storytelling in the processes of social conflicts and their transformation (Lederach 2005; Senehi 2002; Randall 1991; Fine et al. 1992; Anderson 2006; Bar-On et al. 2000; Walker 2015). Scholars have argued that storytelling gives voices to those marginalized and becomes a means through which communities develop and articulate their worldview (Senehi 2002; Narayan 1989; Northrup 1989; Gugelberger and Kearney 1991; Randall 1991). They have claimed that stories create and give expression to personal and group identity and that these stories are a means of socializing people in all cultures (Senehi 2002; Fine et al. 1992; Anderson 2006). Also, they have contended that stories simultaneously engage minds and hearts and encompass the dimension of time, since they can draw on the past in order to envision the future (Senehi 2002; Tonkin 1995; Urban 1991; Bar-On et al. 2000; Belton 2012; Minow 1998). Therefore, with this storytelling approach, the TRC expected to move forward in their goal of reconciliation.

However, unexpected results emerged after five and one-half years of their operation. The statistical data before and after the TRC did not show any significant changes toward the reconciliation in Canada. Before the TRC began, the Canadian Human Rights Commission (2013, 4) found that:

> Aboriginal people living in Canada, compared to non-Aboriginal people, had lower median after-tax income, were more likely to experience unemployment, were more likely to collect employment insurance and social

> assistance, were more likely to live in housing in need of major repairs, were more likely to experience physical, emotional or sexual abuse, were more likely to be victims of violent crimes, and were more likely to be incarcerated and less likely to be granted parole.

Although the TRC process was supposed to address this inequality of the Canadian society, the final report from the Environics Institute for Survey Research (2016a) revealed not very different results from earlier surveys. According to their report, even after the TRC: compared to non-Aboriginal people, Aboriginal people living in Canada experience "discrimination today on a regular basis, comparable to, if not worse than, other marginalized communities in Canada such as Muslims and Black people" (25). Also, the Institute found that they experience systemic discrimination at the institutional level, especially in the education and criminal justice systems (Environics Institute for Survey Research 2016b). In other words, there were no significant differences before and after the TRC, even though the TRC was established to bring constructive changes in Canadian society.

Not only was this failure supported by the statistical data, it was also supported by the arguments of many indigenous groups and scholars (James 2012; Akhtar 2010; Montgomery 2015; Slobodian 2015; Walker 2015). Slobodian (2015) and James (2012) made criticisms that Canadian society is far from being reconciled, since the TRC could not give space for victims and perpetrators to meet, reconcile, and heal with each other. Also, Montgomery (2015) and Akhtar (2010) contended that the TRC failed to address its aim of reconciliation, since it lacked the participation of the non-Aboriginal public. Furthermore, one of the IRS survivors, Viv Ketchum, stated, "I don't expect much to happen after, I don't think . . . We're just going to be placed aside. I think that's the reality for us" (Walker 2015).

Although the TRC should have helped her to feel that justice is being restored and her voice matters in the society, she felt the opposite and was disappointed with the fact that the society still marginalizes Aboriginal people in Canada. Hence, both the statistical data and literature support the conclusion that the TRC failed to transform the conflict and reconcile Aboriginal and non-Aboriginal peoples in Canada.

Research Question

As described above, the conventional wisdom suggests that the TRC should have brought reconciliation to Canadian society, since the TRC used the storytelling method, which is advocated by many scholars because it is very helpful in bringing conflict transformation and reconciliation. Although many Canadians and Aboriginal people expected that the TRC would bring constructive changes and reconciliation to Canadian society, the statistical data, indigenous leaders, and scholars suggest that Aboriginal people are still marginalized, and they feel far from reconciliation. Therefore, in light of this, an important question is: To what extent has the TRC in Canada sought "to get the underlying, root causes of the conflict, to solve the problems that led to it in the first place?" (Avruch 1998, 101). The aim of this research is to answer this question.

In order to do so, I will employ the theoretical framework of conflict transformation. In particular, I will focus on the roles that culture, power, and identity play in conflict transformation and argue that conflict transformation can take place when these three concepts are addressed. For the cultural perspective, I will focus on how inclusive culture can contribute to transforming conflict in society. Regarding power, I will elaborate on how the empowerment of the traditionally oppressed people can contribute to transforming conflict in society. And, for identity, I will describe how renegotiation of identity can contribute to transforming conflict in society as well. Then, I will examine whether the reconciliation efforts by the TRC seek to address the problems through cultural change, empowerment, and identity renegotiation in society (Hallward 2006; Lederach 2003). I will conclude the paper with several implications for scholars and practitioners in the field of reconciliation.

Conceptual Framework: Conflict Transformation

According to Galtung (1969), there are two types of peace: negative peace refers to "the absence of war," and positive peace refers to "a societal condition in which structures of domination and exploitation, which underlie war, have been eliminated" (Avruch 1998, 26). Rooted in Galtung's notion of positive peace, Lederach (1996) emphasizes the notion of conflict transformation (Avruch 1998, 27). Conflict transformation is a process that "engag[es] with and transform[s] the relationships, interests, discourses and, if necessary, the very constitution of society that supports the continuation of . . . conflict" (in Hallward 2006, 49). It aims at addressing "the underlying, root causes of the conflict, to solve the problems that led to it in the first place" (Avruch 1998, 101). Because Lederach and Galtung see that what gave birth to the conflict in the first place is the sociopolitical system (Avruch 1998, 101), they argue that conflict should be approached in wide-ranging and comprehensive ways to progressively "address the surface issues and change underlying social structures and relationship patterns" (Lederach and Maise 2003, 3).

Then, how can we restructure this sociopolitical system? To begin with, Lederach argues that conflict transformation includes "identify[ing] and understand[ing] the cultural patterns that contribute to the rise of violent expressions of conflict" (Lederach and Maise 2003, 4). He emphasizes that there are cultural patterns that are oppressive to those who are traditionally oppressed, and he further maintains that these should be addressed in order for conflict to be transformed, as these are among the root causes of the conflict. Huda et al. (2011) explain these cultural patterns as "a discourse of exclusion of the 'other'" (4). In their article, they recognize the discourse of *othering* as one of the biggest obstacles for the integration of society (Huda et al. 2011, 4). Discourses are developed by those in power with the explicit or implicit aim of shaping attitudes of people to achieve desired goals, which range from legitimizing power to deconstructing power (Aronoff and Kubik 2012). Thus, when discourses continue to exist in society, those without power are oppressed through the language and fixed meaning in codes that are within the discourse. This benefits those with power. Consequently, when this discourse of othering continues to exist, people cannot be integrated in the society and the conflict remains, since one of the root causes that brought the conflict in the first place continues to exist.

The cultural patterns that should be addressed, however, are not only "the discourse of exclusion of the 'other,'" but also the worldviews that are focused only on those with power (Huda et al. 2011, 4; see also Orakzai 2011, 35; Hallward 2006, 51). This point is explained well by Orakzai (2011) and Hallward (2006). In their articles, both point out how societies that have conflict have tried to resolve their conflicts through the approaches developed by Western theory. While analyzing the limitation of these approaches, they both emphasize the importance of incorporating the local culture in conflict transformation. For instance, Orakzai (2011) studied the conflict in the Swat Valley of Pakistan and found that the Pakhtun culture can suggest "ways in which the root cause of the conflict might be addressed to bring about peace and sustainable development," which the Western approaches cannot suggest with the lack of perspective in the region (35). Similarly, Hallward (2006) studied the natural resources conflict regarding the land between Israelis and Palestinians and suggests that scholars and practitioners should look at the conflict reflecting the values, identity, and worldviews of the disputants. In other words, since conflict itself arises from the different worldviews of the disputants, when people try to address the conflict from only one perspective, it lacks the viewpoint of the other disputants who understand causes and dynamics of conflict differently. Thus, in order for conflict to be transformed, structural transformation that integrates indigenous values and draws on indigenous cultural or religious resources must first take place (Orakzai 2011). The cultures of the oppressed ones must be heard and reflected, and people should draw upon the fundamental worldviews of the parties themselves and engage in large cultural change (Hallward 2006).

In addition to explaining these issues in the cultural dimension, Lederach (2005) also points out the issues in the structural dimension that give birth to conflict. He argues that, for society to transform conflict successfully, the cycle of violence that keeps victimizing the victims and benefiting the offenders in the society must be broken (Lederach 2005). As one of the ways to break this cycle, Hallward (2006) maintains those traditionally oppressed must be empowered. Here, she sees empowerment as "a condition in which traditionally disempowered groups have developed their latent power to the point where they can advocate for their own needs and rights" (Hallward 2006, 50). This is similar to Galtung's concept of positive peace as well. Galtung argues that people must pay attention not only to direct violence but also structural violence, which involves "social, political, economic systems which prevent individuals from reaching their human potential" (Hallward 2006, 50; see also Avruch 1998, 26). In other words, for conflict to be transformed, the social, political, and economic systems should not discriminate against any members and should be equally empowering for all members of the society.

Lastly, Lederach (2005) elaborated on the importance of looking at the relational dimensions of the conflict. According to Lederach, the cycle of violence has fixated the interaction and communication between the victims and offenders by breaking up their relationships. When their identity is labeled as victims or offenders in the society, conflict cannot be transformed because these labels prejudice the interactions and communication between them. This is the reason that Lederach claims that the identity and history of victims must be renegotiated within the society by engaging all members of the society. The victims' and offenders' identities must be integrated together to include all of them. In remembering the history and renegotiating the identity with all members of the society, "the proximity that touches the web of community life in context of actual relationship and community" can be developed, and the healing process can finally take place in the society (Lederach 2005, 145). Thus, reconnecting people in actual relationships—"practices of accessibility"—is the core issue that can decide the success of restorative justice as well as conflict transformation (Lederach 2005, 143). Consequently, the society needs to help restructure identities of those traditionally marginalized in global and local contexts (Huda et al. 2011).

As illustrated above, the conceptual framework—conflict transformation—suggests that when all of these happen, constructive social change and genuine reconciliation can take place in the society. Then, what about the TRC in Canada? Did the TRC seek to address the root causes of the conflict through inclusive culture, empowerment, and identity renegotiation in the society? To answer this question, I examined the TRC employing the previously mentioned elements.

Data and Analysis

The TRC in Canada is unique compared to the TRC in other societies. Although the TRC in other societies, such as South Africa, Sierra Leone, and Liberia, emerged "from a process of transition to democracy or from a pact among previously warring parties," the TRC in Canada emerged simply because of a court mandate (James 2012, 189; Stanton 2011, 4). In 2005, approximately 15,000 residential school survivors filed a class action suit against the Canadian federal government, and, as one of the conditions of their settlement agreement, the court mandated the establishment of the TRC. This was because people expected that "the TRC would help mainstream Canada to better understand the actions and consequences of residential schools and allow aboriginal victims an outlet to express their feelings and pain" (Montgomery 2015).

After years of preparation on how to bring reconciliation to the Canadian society, the TRC employed the victim-centered approach, which uses storytelling as a method to reconciliation, adopted from the successful model of the TRC in South Africa (Slobodian 2015; James 2012). From June 2010, the TRC travelled the country to hear testimony from 7,000 witnesses about their experiences at residential schools in its five and a half years of operations (Walker 2015). During this process, the TRC focused on addressing three specific goals: acknowledging and witnessing the Indian Residential School experience, promoting awareness of the IRS system and its impacts, and creating a public record of the IRS legacy (Stanton 2011). Then, which of the elements—inclusive culture, empowerment, and the renegotiation of identity—has the TRC addressed?

Firstly, the TRC failed to foster inclusive culture in the Canadian society. It could not address "the discourse of exclusion of the 'other'" (Huda et al. 2011, 4). Also, it could not include the worldview of Aboriginal people in its process. According to James, although "the discursive frames promoted by the Canadian government and media must be addressed" for conflict to be transformed, these deeply rooted aspects were *not* addressed during the TRC process (James 2012, 197). According to James, instead of addressing the prevailing anti-indigenous stereotypes and biases, the TRC process further strengthened the stereotypes and biases against Aboriginal people. After the terrible experiences in the IRS were shared, the Canadian media often projected the IRS survivors as "helpless therapeutic subjects who need externally administered healing in order to unburden themselves of their anger and become conventionally productive citizens" (James 2012, 197). In other words, although the storytelling process was supposed to bring Aboriginal and non-Aboriginal peoples together, it ended up highlighting the differences between Aboriginal and non-Aboriginal peoples and fed into the discourse of othering. And this discourse again benefited those with power by helping to ignore the important question of "political self-determination and control of land" of Aboriginal people (James 2012, 197; Henderson and Wakeham 2009, 4).

Not only did it fail to address the discourse of othering, the TRC also failed to include the worldview of Aboriginal people in Canada. Although the TRC was established in the context that the culture of Aboriginal people has been suppressed and missed for almost a century, the TRC did not hear and reflect the fundamental values and worldviews of Aboriginal people as it was supposed to (Henderson and Wakeham 2009). In the TRC project, what Aboriginal people wanted were disclosure, information about what went wrong, explanations, apologies, and the assurance that changes will be made so that it does not happen again (Carroll and Unger 2015). However, the TRC ignored what they wanted. Disclosure and information about what went wrong, explanation, and assurance about the future were not included in the process (Carroll and Unger 2015). Only a collective apology was given by the Canadian government in 2008 (Edwards 2010). Lederach argues that, for conflict to be transformed and for restorative justice to take place, the society needs to "create adequate public truth and accountability" (2005, 143). However, the TRC only focused on creating public truth, not accountability. Instead, the TRC (2015) framed this accountability as "the shaming and pointing out wrongdoing" and stated that these were not the purpose of the TRC (vi). James (2012) criticized this by comparing it to a situation in which perpetrators say, "We are sorry for what happened to them," not "We are sorry for what we did," since this missed the necessity of accountability in promoting restorative justice (203). Accordingly, the TRC did not reflect the perspectives of Aboriginal people about how they would like to transform this conflict.

Secondly, the TRC failed to empower the traditionally oppressed. Although the structural issues that oppress Aboriginal people must have been addressed to break the cycle of violence, the TRC did not pay attention to this aspect at all. The issues often brought by Aboriginal scholars and practitioners are the self-governing nation and land rights (Rymhs 2006; Akhtar 2010). They often argue that these issues must be addressed, since the denial of these rights is what actually resulted in giving birth to the IRS system and leading the society to support this system a century ago (Simpson 2001; James 2012). However, even after a century, in 2016, these political and economic rights were still not recognized in Canada. To illustrate: Although the Constitution Act of 1982 recognizes the First Nations as a minority, it does not actually set out any specific guarantees of their self-determination (Akhtar 2010). Also, in 2007, although many states adopted the Indigenous Declaration of Rights at the United Nations, the Canadian government still declined to adopt this declaration. Power is still dominated by the government and the individual beneficiaries of the injustice (James 2012; Akhtar 2010). Although the IRS, which used to explicitly discriminate against and oppress Aboriginal people, was abolished, the sociopolitical systems that implicitly carry out the power imbalances between Aboriginal and non-Aboriginal peoples continue, while non-Aboriginal people still do not recognize the political and economic rights of Aboriginal people in the society (Stanton 2011; Akhtar 2010). Therefore, restorative justice and equality could not be brought to the society. Again, this contributed to the failure of the TRC in bringing constructive changes to the system that reinforces the power imbalance in Canada.

Lastly, the TRC failed to help Aboriginal people renegotiate their identity in their society. The identity of the traditionally marginalized is often renegotiated in the process of storytelling because it gives voices to everyone regardless of age, space, time, and intellectual level and enables people to remember, emphasize, and accept the reality of Aboriginal people and build the future together based on the present (Senehi 2002). However, what the TRC did through their storytelling process was simply to hear the voices of Aboriginal people and write them down in the report (James 2012). No effort was made beyond this simple storytelling process. There was no shared empathy between Aboriginal and non-Aboriginal people, because there was negligible involvement of the non-Aboriginal public (Stanton 2011). Also, the reality of Aboriginal people was not recognized as reality, since media only focused on sharing the provocative stories—because the more tragic the survivors' experiences were, the more likely news was to gain attention (Stanton 2011; James 2012). Because the TRC did not use the storytelling method correctly, the TRC just contributed to inheriting and internalizing the dichotomies of the "oppressor and oppressed" even further (Rymhs 2006). Aboriginal "identity and history often dwell on tragic narratives rather than on the ways that Aboriginal people have re-imagined themselves in the present" (Rymhs 2006, 118). The renegotiation of Canadian identity to include those marginalized through "restory[ing]" the past and future in the present did not take place (Lederach 2005, 140); and, unfortunately, the TRC could not bring changes to the imperial legacy and national identity when it did not recognize the identity of Aboriginal people in Canada as well (Rymhs 2006).

Accordingly, although the TRC argued that the Commission's focus was to "lay the foundation for . . . reconciliation," the TRC did not lay any foundation for reconciliation (TRC 2015, vi). They did not foster inclusive culture by addressing the discourse of othering and including the values and worldviews of Aboriginal people in transforming the conflict. They did not empower the Aboriginal people, as they failed to recognize the political and economic rights of the Aboriginal people. Also, they failed to help them renegotiate their identity in the Canadian society, since they could not go beyond the storytelling process, though this was the most important part of the process. Therefore, the TRC failed to bring about constructive social changes to the sociopolitical system that gave birth to the conflict in the first place and failed to transform the conflict, resulting in a failure to bring genuine reconciliation between Aboriginal and non-Aboriginal peoples.

Conclusion and Implications

As many scholars have noted, constructive social change began in Canada when a collective apology was given and people started uncovering the truth (Edwards 2010; Carroll and Unger 2015; Bombay et al. 2013). However, further meaningful constructive social change will not happen with only this collective apology. For the society to change, the meaningful participation of all members of the society is needed, since it requires them to change the culture and to renegotiate the identity of non-Aboriginal people in the society. During this process, people need to recognize the sociopolitical systems that have oppressed certain groups of people so that the society may move toward the justice and equality of all people.

The statement of one of the Aboriginal scholars well emphasizes this point: he claims that the conflict in Canada will be transformed "when the dominant society respects and recognizes [Aboriginal people] as peoples, honors [their] treaties to their full meaning and intent, acknowledges [their] land rights and treats [them] with the same respect any self-governing Nation would expect" (Simpson 2001, 145). For Aboriginals to be respected and recognized as a people, the culture and society in Canada must include them and give them a new identity other than that of being the victims. Also, for their treaties and land rights to be recognized and honored, the sociopolitical systems and discourses that have oppressed them must be understood and addressed.

This is what the TRC overlooked in this reconciliation process: storytelling does not automatically foster inclusive culture, empower those marginalized, and help those marginalized to renegotiate their identity. What the TRC should have focused on was that they needed not just storytelling but the storytelling that could bring about all these elements. From the beginning of the project, the TRC was supposed to reflect the values and worldviews of Aboriginal people and recognize how the discourses and sociopolitical systems have marginalized them. Then, based on this understanding, they were supposed to build a project plan. However, what the TRC did in their planning process was to look for a successful model and simply adopt what the TRC in South Africa did in a different context of the society. Also, even during the process, the Canadian TRC should not have stopped at the level of only giving voices to the survivors and listening to their stories. They were supposed to invite non-Aboriginal public into the process as well and make an effort to integrate them through the process. In other words, the failure of the TRC lies in the shallow understanding of how storytelling can bring about constructive changes to the society and the hasty delivery of them based on this superficial understanding.

From this process, scholars and practitioners in the field of reconciliation can learn lessons. They need to understand the important roles that culture, power, and identity play in conflict transformation and reconciliation. When developing any reconciliation policies or project, they should begin with looking inward at all levels of perspectives and engage and respect the worldview of those traditionally marginalized to change their reality (Cherubini and Hodson 2008). Instead of assuming the needs and values of those marginalized, scholars and practitioners should start asking questions, such as how those marginalized feel about the process and what they expect to happen through the process, and they should be involved in the designing process. Then, scholars and practitioners would be able to recognize how those marginalized have been oppressed and marginalized through the sociopolitical systems and discourses. Also, when the project is implemented, scholars and practitioners must ensure that this process should not only focus on healing those marginalized but also on integrating all members in the society by encouraging active participation of all. The wounds of the wronged cannot be fully healed without pulling out the thorn together with the wrongdoers, since the responsibility for changing the realities of those marginalized does not rest solely on the TRC or those marginalized.

Bibliography

"87% of Canadians believe aboriginal people experience discrimination: Survey." *Global News* (Canada), June 8, 2016. http://globalnews.ca/news/2749567/87-of-canadians-believe-aboriginal-people-experience-discrimination-survey/.

Akhtar, Zia. 2010. "Canadian Genocide and Official Culpability." *International Criminal Law Review,* 10 (1): 111–135.

Anderson, Benedict. 2006. *Imagined Communities: Reflections on the Origin and Spread of Nationalism,* rev. ed. New York: Verso.

Aronoff, Myron J., and Jan Kubik. 2012. *Anthropology and Political Science: A Convergent Approach.* New York: Berghahn Books.

Avruch, Kevin. 1998. *Culture and Conflict Resolution.* Washington, DC: US Institute of Peace Press.

Bar-On, Dan, Susanne Kutz, and Dirk Wegner. 2000. *Bridging the Gap: Storytelling as a Way to Work through Political and Collective Hostilities.* Hamburg: Körber-Stiftung.

Belton, Neil. 2012. *The Good Listener: Helen Bamber; A Life against Cruelty.* London: Faber and Faber.

Bombay, Amy, Kimberley Matheson, and Hymie Anisman. 2013. "Expectations Among Aboriginal Peoples in Canada Regarding the Potential Impacts of a Government Apology." *Political Psychology* 34 (3): 443–460.

Canadian Human Rights Commission. 2013. *Report on Equality Rights of Aboriginal People.* Retrieved from http://chrc-ccdp.gc.ca/sites/default/files/equality_aboriginal_report.pdf.

Carroll, Robyn, Christopher To, and Marc Unger. 2015. "Apology Legislation and Its Implications for International Dispute Resolution." *Dispute Resolution International,* 9 (2):115–138.

Cherubini, Lorenzo, and John Hodson. 2008. "Ontario Ministry of Education Policy and Aboriginal Learners' Epistemologies: A Fundamental Disconnect." *Canadian Journal of Educational Administration and Policy* 79: 1–33.

Edwards, Jason A. 2010. "Apologizing for the Past for a Better Future: Collective Apologies in the United States, Australia, and Canada." *Southern Communication Journal* 75 (1): 57–75.

Environics Institute for Survey Research. 2016a. *Canadian Public Opinion on Aboriginal Peoples: Final Report.* https://www.environicsinstitute. org/docs/default-source/project-documents/public-opinion-about-aboriginal-issues-in-canada-2016/final-report.pdf.

The Environics Institute for Survey Research. 2016b. "New Survey Reveals How Mainstream Society Views Aboriginal Peoples in Canada." http://www.environicsinstitute.org/docs/default-source/project-documents/public-opinion-about-aboriginal-issues-in-canada-2016/ canadian-public-opinion-on-aboriginal-peoples---media-release-english---june-6-2016.pdf.

Fine, Elizabeth C., and Jean Haskell. 1992. *Performance, Culture, and Identity.* Westport, CT: Praeger.

Galtung, Johan, 1969. "Violence, Peace, and Peace Research." *Journal of Peace Research* 6 (3): 167–191.

Gugelberger, Georg, and Michael Kearney. 1991. "Voices for the Voiceless: Testimonial Literature in Latin America." *Latin American Perspectives* 18 (3): 3–14.

Hallward, Maia Carter 2006. "Natural Resource Transformation: Incorporating Identity." *Journal of Peacebuilding and Development* 3 (1): 48–62.

Henderson, Jennifer, and Pauline Wakeham. 2009. "Colonial Reckoning, National Reconciliation?: Aboriginal Peoples and the Culture of Redress in Canada." *ESC: English Studies in Canada* 35 (1): 1–26.

Huda, Qamar-Ul, Mohammed Abu-Nimer, Amr Qader, and Erin McCandless. 2011. "Islam, Peacebuilding and Development." *Journal of Peacebuilding and Development* 6 (1): 1–5.

James, Matt. 2012. "A Carnival of Truth? Knowledge, Ignorance and the Canadian Truth and Reconciliation Commission." *International Journal of Transitional Justice* 6 (2): 182–204.

Lederach, John Paul. 1996. *Preparing for Peace: Conflict Transformation across Cultures.* Syracuse, NY: Syracuse University Press.

Lederach, John Paul. 2003. "Conflict Transformation." *Beyond Intractability*. Eds. Guy Burgess and Heidi Burgess. Conflict Information Consortium, University of Colorado, Boulder. http://www.beyondintractability.org/essay/transformation.

Lederach, John Paul. 2005. *The Moral Imagination: The Art and Soul of Building Peace*. Oxford: Oxford University Press.

Lederach, J., and M. Maise. 2003. "Conflict Transformation." http://peacebuildingforlanguagelearners.pbworks.com/w/file/fetch/73426a925/Lederach%20and%20Maiese_Conflict%20Transformation.pdf.

MacDonald, David B., and Graham Hudson. 2012. "The Genocide Question and Indian Residential Schools in Canada." *Canadian Journal of Political Science* 45 (2): 427–449.

Miller, James R. 2004. *Lethal Legacy: Current Native Controversies in Canada*. Toronto: McClelland and Stewart.

Minow, Martha. 1998. *Between Vengeance and Forgiveness: Facing History after Genocide and Mass Violence*. Boston: Beacon Press.

Montgomery, Marc. 2015. "Canada's Truth and Reconciliation Commission Ends." *Radio Canada International*, June 1, 2015. http://www.rcinet.ca/en/2015/06/01/canadas-truth-and-reconciliation-commission-ends/.

Narayan, Kirin. 1989. *Storytellers, Saints, and Scoundrels: Folk Narrative in Hindu Religious Teaching*. Philadelphia: University of Pennsylvania Press.

Northrup, Terrell A. 1989. "The Dynamic of Identity in Personal and Social Conflict." In *Intractable Conflicts and Their Transformation*, edited by Louis Kriesberg, Terrell A. Northrup, and Stuart J. Thorson, 55–82. Syracuse, NY: Syracuse University Press.

Orakzai, Saira Bano. 2011. "Conflict in the Swat Valley of Pakistan: Pakhtun Culture and Peacebuilding Theory-Practice Application." *Journal of Peacebuilding and Development* 6 (1): 35–48.

Randall, Margaret. 1991. "Reclaiming Voices: Notes on a New Female Practice in Journalism." *Latin American Perspectives* 18 (3): 103–113.

Robertson, Kirsty. 2009. "Threads of Hope: The Living Healing Quilt Project." *ESC: English Studies in Canada* 35 (1): 85–107.

Royal Commission on Aboriginal Peoples. 1996. *Looking Forward, Looking Back.* Vol. 1 of *Report of the Royal Commission on Aboriginal Peoples.* https://www.bac-lac.gc.ca/eng/discover/aboriginal-heritage/royal-commission-aboriginal-peoples/Pages/final-report.aspx.

Rymhs, Deena. 2006. "Appropriating Guilt: Reconciliation in an Aboriginal Canadian Context." *ESC: English Studies in Canada* 32 (1): 105–123.

Saunders, Harold H. 1999. *A Public Peace Process: Sustained Dialogue to Transform Racial and Ethnic Conflicts.* New York: St. Martin's Press.

Senehi, Jessica. 2002. "Constructive Storytelling: A Peace Process." *Peace and Conflict Studies* 9 (2): 41–63.

Simpson, Leanne. 2001. "Aboriginal Peoples and Knowledge: Decolonizing Our Processes." *Canadian Journal of Native Studies* 21 (1): 137–148.

Slobodian, Mayana C. "Canada's Truth Commission on Residential Schools Is Coming to a Troubling Close." *Vice*, May 25, 2015. http://www.vice.com/en_ca/read/canadas-truth-commission-on-residential-schools-is-coming-to-a-troubling-close-far-from-reconciliation.

Stanton, Kim. 2011. "Canada's Truth and Reconciliation Commission: Settling the Past?" *International Indigenous Policy Journal* 2 (3): 1–18.

Tonkin, Elizabeth. 1995. *Narrating Our Pasts: The Social Construction of Oral History.* Cambridge: Cambridge University Press.

Truth and Reconciliation Commission of Canada. 2008. *Indian Residential Schools: An Overview.* http://www.trc.ca/assets/pdf/mroom_ResidentialSchoolsPamplet_en_dec11.2.pdf

Truth and Reconciliation Commission of Canada. 2015. *Honouring the Truth, Reconciling for the Future: Summary of the Final Report of the Truth and Reconciliation Commission of Canada.* http://nctr.ca/assets/reports/Final%20Reports/Executive_Summary_English_Web.pdf.

United Nations. 1948. Convention on the Prevention and Punishment of the Crime of Genocide. https://treaties.un.org/doc/Publication/UNTS/Volume%2078/volume-78-i-1021-english.pdf

Urban, Greg. 1991. *A Discourse-Centered Approach to Culture: Native South American Myths and Rituals.* Austin: University of Texas Press.

Walker, Connie. 2015. "Truth and Reconciliation: Aboriginal People Conflicted as Commission Wraps Up after 6 Years." *CBC News*, June 1, 2015. http://www.cbc.ca/news/indigenous/truth-and-reconciliation-aboriginal-people-conflicted-as-commission-wraps-up-after-6-years-1.3094753.

Woolford, Andrew John. 2009. "Ontological Destruction: Genocide and Canadian Aboriginal Peoples." *Genocide Studies and Prevention* 4 (1): 81–97.

CHAPTER 4

Becoming Manjaco: Immigration, Integration, and Identity in Cabo Verde, West Africa

Brandon D. Lundy and Kezia Darkwah

On January 23, 2012, Resolution No. 3 enacted the National Immigration Strategy for the island nation of Cabo Verde, the first of its kind in the country. As a buffer nation to Western Europe with a rapidly developing economy and good governance indicators, Cabo Verde is transitioning from a sending to a receiving nation for African mainlanders. A one-month ethnographic investigation among Bissau-Guinean labor migrants demonstrates how communities undergoing immigration pressures react to outsiders in complex ways. Hosts sometimes engage politics of identity to denigrate labor migrants when they perceive resource limitations. While a majority of the Bissau-Guineans had stable, full-time work, started families, and joined community organizations, frictions, especially between disenfranchised domestic youth and migrants, sometimes intensified intergroup hostility observable as prejudice, discrimination, and violence. These sentiments seemed to lessen when local institutions had the capacity to welcome and integrate visitors, uphold and revise laws, and create cooperative strategies around education, development, and security.

The Manjaco

Ethnographer Eric Gable (2006) once described the Manjaco ethnic group of the Upper Guinea Coast as "quintessentially West African," working as "the first labor migrants in the region that comprises the Casamance (in Southern Senegal), the Gambia, and the rivers of Guinea-Bissau" (387). As noted in early European accounts of the coast, "Manjaco typically worked as sailors or stevedores for Portuguese merchants" (Gable 2006, 388), even learning their language and self-identifying as Portuguese throughout the region. According to Gable, Manjaco were a significant presence throughout colonial urban enclaves and, "To this day, Manjaco tend to migrate as laborers . . . in the lower rungs of the ladder in the cities of West Africa and Europe" (388). Alba and Foner (2014) refer to these types of migrants as "low status"—or those having low levels of education, low paying jobs, and often stigmatized in host communities because of this background. The Manjaco number approximately 300,000 worldwide, making up 8.3% of Guinea-Bissau's population of 1.5 million today.

When conducting survey research among Bissau-Guinean labor migrants in Cabo Verde, five of the 57 surveyed were from the Manjaco ethnic group (8.77%), while other respondents self-identified as Fula (15), Papel (9), Mandinga (9), Balanta (8), Mancanha (6), and Other (5). Interestingly, the local population referred to many of these non-Manjaco labor migrants as Manjaco as well. According to one respondent, "One sign of bigotry that is quite common [in Cabo Verde] is when the locals call us Manjaco. The first arrival of Bissau-Guineans in Cabo Verde belonged to the Manjack ethnic group. After that, everyone else who comes from the West African mainland is referred to as Manjaco in the pejorative sense" (May 17, 2015). This chapter considers why many African labor migrants in Cabo Verde are "becoming Manjaco" and what this might mean for their prospects of successful community integration.

Cabo Verde

The well-known Africanist Basil Davidson once described the island nation of Cabo Verde as the "fortunate isles" (1989). His description was partially ironic as "a barren land where people, as their poets say, have learned to feed on stones: the goats have taught them how" (5). Davidson was also in awe of the people's perseverance in the face of deprivation, political successes against all odds, and strong spirit able to embrace a barrage of contradictions. According to Davidson, "The Cape Verde islands have long been an archipelago of emigration for reasons anything but fortunate. . . . Drought and famine have driven the people away. . . . they are 'waiting to depart' so that, while cheerfulness keeps breaking in, there is an air of sorrow to the place" (7).

The volcanic archipelago is located 310 miles from Senegal's West African Coast, set adrift out in the Atlantic. With a land mass of only 1,577 square miles, partitioned among ten islands and a population of 505,000, "Today, more people with origins in Cabo Verde live outside the country than inside it" (BBC News 2016). The story goes that, while the islands were known to mainlanders who used them as temporary fishing sites from time to time, no permanent settlements were ever established until 1462, when Portuguese settlers arrived on the island of São Tiago. Ribeira Grande (later renamed Cidade Velha and inscribed as a UNESCO World Heritage Site in 2009 as Europe's first colonial outpost in the tropics) was established as a strategic settlement in the trade of firearms, rum, and cloth for enslaved peoples, ivory, gold, and salt. By 1495, Cabo Verde became a Portuguese crown colony that administered both its own territory and the adjacent mainland of "Portuguese Guinea," present day Guinea-Bissau.

These sister republics rebelled against the Portuguese under the leadership of agronomist Amilcar Cabral, with many Cabo Verdeans joining the liberation war in Guinea-Bissau by 1960. With the

Carnation Revolution in Portugal on April 25, 1974, when the Estado Novo regime was overthrown, these two West African territories won independence and were granted UN membership by 1975. Soon after, the conditions worsened in Guinea-Bissau due to an ongoing drought and racial tensions between the black population of Guinea-Bissau and the mulatto population of Cabo Verde. On November 14, 1980, João Bernardo "Nino" Vieira, a highly respected member of the African Party for the Independence of Guinea and Cape Verde (PAIGC) and a key figure in the war against Portuguese colonial rule, toppled the unified government of Luis Cabral, Amilcar's half-brother, in a bloodless coup. By 1992, a new constitution brought a multi-party system to Cabo Verde, which has been dominated by two parties ever since, the African party for the Independence of Cape Verde (PAICV) and the Movement for Democracy (MpD), while Guinea-Bissau has rarely seen an elected president serve out a fully-mandated term in office (Lundy 2012).

To summarize, "Poor in natural resources, prone to drought and with little arable land, the Cabo Verde islands have won a reputation for achieving political and economic stability" (BBC News 2016). Guinea-Bissau, on the other hand, remains mired in political uncertainty, underdevelopment, and poverty, leaving many to seek their livelihoods outside of the country.

Regional Integration

As Davidson noted, for much of its history, Cabo Verde has been a country of emigration, with large diasporas springing up in the United States, Europe, and the West African region. By 2007, however, the West African route into the Spanish Canary Islands from Cabo Verde was blocked due to a bilateral agreement with Spain, including a repatriation clause and the installment of the SIVE maritime surveillance system. According to the World Bank net migration indicator, which is the total number of immigrants less the annual number of emigrants, Cabo Verde went from –25.866 migrants/1,000 population in 2007 to –11.052 migrants/1,000 population by 2012 (World Bank Group 2017). This is a clear indicator of fewer people leaving, more people coming in, or, more likely, both. Also in 2007, Cabo Verde was promoted from least developed country to developing country status by the United Nations based on improving economic conditions, thus making it more enticing to economic migrants from throughout the region. Furthermore, Cabo Verde validated the Economic Community of West African States (ECOWAS) *Protocol of Free Movement of Persons and the Right of Residence and Establishment*, although, by 2008, they had also enacted a new Labour Code that "introduced a law that only foreigners in legal status have the right to work" (Varela and Barbosa 2014, 459). Therefore, while migrants have the right to enter Cabo Verde for up to 90 days, those that overstay violate this Labour Code and become irregular migrants left unprotected, what Pedro Marcelino referred to as denizens (2016), trapped in what Stef Jansen calls "zones of humiliating entrapment" (2009).

Rising Immigration and Tension

Once a transit country for potential Europe-bound immigrants, Cabo Verde has now been described as a "buffer nation" for the West and a "final destination" for labor migrants due to these new restrictions and tourism investments (Marcelino 2011; Varela and Barbosa 2014, 451). Data supplied by the Cabo Verdean National Statistics Institute for 2013 listed 17,788 immigrants that year, 3,961 (22%; 3,243 male, 718 females) of which came from Guinea-Bissau, the most from any sending country. Overall, people residing in Cabo Verde representing other nationalities now make up about 3% of the total population (Varela and Barbosa 2014, 454), while the island of Boa

Vista's population of 8,698 (2010) is made up of 22% (1,942) foreign guests. This dramatic rise in immigrant populations has led to increased tension between local hosts and foreign guests in some communities. For example, on October 5, 2010, a headline decried, "Boa Vista get to the streets for peace after a brutal murder." According to the story,

> Boa Vista has witnessed the biggest demonstration in its history. The Guinean community, people from every island in Cape Verde, Europeans living on the island of dunes, tourists, all united in the March for Peace, a response of love and hope for an episode that stunned Boa Vista: the brutal murder of a Guinean citizen in the heart of the capital and the subsequent revolt of their community. A case that exposed the social weaknesses in the first tourist island of the archipelago. The City Council has already warned that it will be "more selective" in the granting of residence permits. (Valdigem 2010)

This incident and others like it led to a number of local and national initiatives aimed at abating this increasing community tension, including the enactment of Resolution No. 3, the National Immigration Strategy for the island nation of Cabo Verde, on January 23, 2012, the first of its kind in the country.

Politics of Identity (Becoming Other)

The politics of identity create complex feelings about others, those who are different from oneself in a way that has been determined to be meaningful; and then these feelings are often acted upon in either helpful or harmful ways (Appiah 2006). These sentimentalities toward the other can change over time from feelings of receptivity and belongingness to alienation and othering expressed through feelings of prejudice and discrimination toward an outgroup that can accompany intergroup hostilities (Baumeister and Vohs 2007; Campbell 1965; Jackson 1993). Triggers to intergroup hostilities can be perceived or real shortages of valued resources such as jobs, while positive relations can be achieved through shared values and goals, such as security and community development. One of my favorite quotes expressing these sentiments is from Chuck Frake (2006, 41), who writes,

> A major motive in human life,[1] on occasion not even second to survival, is the need to be somebody. To be somebody, one must have recognition from one's fellows. Violence, by threatening survival, one's own as well as others', provides a sure route to recognition. But who are one's fellows? Who are those like you? And who are the "others," those to whose fate one can be indifferent? . . . These are the issues from the individual perspective. From the wider social and political perspective one must ask, what are the conditions of conflict and what are the available resources for identity construction? And, historically, how did these particular conditions and re-sources come to be at hand? Fully appreciating the power of each of these perspectives (agentive, structural, and historical) within a single account is the necessary but elusive goal of any proper social theory.

Conflicts abound in the context of immigration in Cabo Verde. Dilemmas around belongingness and difference are complicated when discussing Bissau-Guinean labor migrants in Cabo Verde, where a shared language and historical context overlap with racial difference and economic disparities. What results is a complex scene where identities directly affect livelihoods, security, and feelings of belongingness or discrimination.

Findings of Conflict ("Becoming Manjaco")

In May and June of 2015, we surveyed 57 Bissau-Guinean immigrants on the islands of Boa Vista and Santiago, islands with two of the three largest immigrant communities in the country. These migrants worked in service and construction, and some attended school. Twenty-four (24) of the 57 respondents had resided in Cabo Verde for more than ten years, with the average age at the time of migration being 25.6. Respondents' average salary was $3,422 dollars, close to the average GDP per capita (PPP) of $3,800 (2008 est.) in Cabo Verde and well above the same in Guinea-Bissau, which was only $600 (2008 est.). Respondent remittances averaged $1,007.45 per year. When asked if they had ever experienced intolerance, prejudice, or discrimination in Cabo Verde, 41 of 57 Bissau-Guinean respondents said that they had. Furthermore, 26 of 57 felt insecure or extremely insecure when it came to their personal safety. Ten (10) of the 57 survey respondents mentioned the term "manjaco" as a derogatory label used against them as an African mainlander with darker skin.

The ethnic Manjack are considered one of the earliest peoples to come to Cabo Verde in conjunction with the Portuguese in the 1500s, sometimes in their employ and others as their captives. Today, the word expresses a marker of difference. These perceived markers of difference are enacted and sometimes even escalated to violence. For example, one respondent recounted, "On May 10, 2014, a Bissau-Guinean security guard on his way to work was assaulted by three men who were trying to provoke him and take what he had on his person. He didn't respond, and they shot him in the face where he ended up losing an eye" (May 17, 2015). During a focus group discussion with the leadership of the Guinean Association of Boavista (May 24, 2015), they described a similar violent event, "We can recall a serious conflict that happened in 2002, when Guineans brawled with locals from Santiago. During the fight, a Guinean got stabbed. . . . We were afraid that he was going to die, and there was no hospital."

Another example from a Bissau-Guinean woman who sold hamburgers out of her shipping container storefront said, "Where I sell hamburgers, people are sometimes drunk. They always try to get stuff from me on credit, and sometimes I cannot accept that. They then start to insult me by saying, 'Ah don't forget, you are Manjaco. You think you are an important person, but you are not.' I just try and let it go" (May 22, 2015). These rising tensions between these neighbors, usually made up of disenfranchised urban youth from the capital city of Praia, the local community, and immigrants from the mainland, have transformed the country's socio-cultural milieu. To illustrate, researcher Derek Pardue wrote, "By 2007 the term *kaçubodi*, the Kriolu pronunciation of 'cash or body,' had become a catch all phrase to describe the rise of urban violence" (2016, 333). Survey respondents, when referencing their fear related to personal security and rising crime rates, particularly muggings and youth gang activity, also regularly used this phrase.

According to some, however, these incidents of discrimination have lessened since 2012 when a national plan was put into place to help resolve tensions resulting from immigration pressures. According to our interview with the police chief of Boa Vista,

> The statistics on crime rates on the island are very low and have decreased significantly between 2012 and 2014. But something bad will happen and the whole perception of safety will go down. The most recent incident of note was when a member of the Guinean immigrant community was assaulted by a youth from Praia. Thousands of immigrants gathered in front of the suspected perpetrator's house. I believe this event went down without

incident because I had established rapport with the community. (May 25, 2015)

The Immigration Policy

The findings of this study are very much in line with those expressed in Resolution 3, the National Immigration Strategy (2012). This policy opens with the following statement:

> Cape Verde is considered, mainly starting from independence, a country of immigration, with the entry of immigrants from Europe, Asia, and the West African Coast. The causes identified are the political and social stability of Cape Verde, its geographical position at the crossroads of three continents, the dynamic of economic growth, the regional integration in ECOWAS pursuant to the ratification of the treaties and conventions they respect, as well as the bilateral and multilateral accords kept internationally. (translated by Lisa C. Smith)

This immigration policy now inscribes the adoption of measures to combat discrimination and the violation of the rights of migrants by training officials and by creating campaigns to influence public opinion about common misconceptions around migration (Lartey and Lundy 2017). Recognizing that the integration of immigrants into society is one of Cabo Verde's most important challenges, this policy acknowledges,

> Integration is a dynamic and bi-directional process of including immigrants in institutions and in the host society. To overcome barriers, the host society and immigrants must engage in a mutual process of integration. The promotion of fundamental rights, non-discrimination, and equality of opportunities for all are fundamental aspects. (Cabo Verde National Immigration Strategy 2012, 24; translated by Lisa C. Smith)

Furthermore, the policy promotes access to labor markets, education, housing, social protection, and healthcare, along with encouraging coexistence of citizens belonging to different religions and cultures. During our fieldwork, we witnessed and later wrote about these community changes in action, including the building of affordable housing, literacy campaigns, intercultural events at schools, effective community policing, amnesty periods, and the opening of national and municipal-level immigration offices (Lartey and Lundy 2017).

Conclusion

Finding common ground is one way to avoid intolerance, prejudice, and discrimination. For Bissau-Guinean immigrants and Cabo Verdean hosts, there is a lot of fertile ground to find similarities. To name just a few, there is a common history including a shared colonial experience and independence movement, a common language, geographic proximity, and the necessity to seek a livelihood far from home. The politics of identity remain a powerful motivator of negativity in Cabo Verde around racial and religious differences and a lack of resources, including high unemployment rates (12.4% in 2015, down from a high of 16.8% in 2012). Active and sustained mitigation on the part of the national and local governments, non-governmental organizations, and local community associations, however, are having a clear effect on both local receptivity and foreign guests' community integration. Through these initiatives throughout Cabo Verde, instead of the immigrant others becoming Manjaco, they are trusted neighbors instead.

Bibliography

Alba, Richard, and Nancy Foner. 2014. "Comparing Immigrant Integration in North America and Western Europe: How Much Do the Grand Narratives Tell Us?" *International Migration Review* 48 (S1): S263–S291.

Appiah, Kwame Anthony. 2006. "The Politics of Identity." *Daedalus* 135 (4): 15–22.

Baumeister, Roy F., and Kathleen D. Vohs. 2007. "Realistic Group Conflict Theory." *Encyclopedia of Social Psychology* 2: 725–726. Los Angeles: Sage.

BBC News. 2016. "Cabo Verde Country Profile." Accessed October 16, 2016. http://www.bbc.com/news/world-africa-13148486.

Cabo Verde National Immigration Strategy. 2012. *Estratégia Nacional de Imigração: Resolução No. 3/2012 de 23 de Janeiro.* Cabo Verde: Unidade de Coordenação da Imigração.

Campbell, Donald T. 1965. "Ethnocentric and Other Altruistic Motives." In *Nebraska Symposium on Motivation, 1965*, Lincoln, NE: University of Nebraska Press.

Davidson, Basil. 1989. *The Fortunate Isles: A Study in African Transformation.* Trenton, NJ: Africa World Press.

Frake, Charles O. 2006. "Abu Sayyaf: Displays of Violence and the Proliferation of Contested Identities among Philippine Muslims." *American Anthropologist* 100 (1): 41–54.

Gable, Eric. 2006. "The Funeral and Modernity in Manjaco." *Cultural Anthropology* 21 (3): 385–415.

INECV. 2013. *Portal de dados Cabo Verde.* Instituto Nacional de Estatística. Accessed October 18, 2016. http://capeverde.africadata.org/.

Jackson, Jay W. 1993. "Realistic Group Conflict Theory: A Review and Evaluation of the Theoretical and Empirical Literature." *Psychological Record* 43 (3): 395–415.

Jansen, Stef. 2009. "After the Red Passport: Towards an Anthropology of the Everyday Geopolitics of Entrapment in the EU's 'Immediate Outside.'" *Journal of the Royal Anthropological Institute* 15 (4): 815–832.

Lartey, Kezia, and Brandon D. Lundy. 2017. "Policy Considerations Regarding the Integration of Lusophone West African Immigrant Populations." *Border Crossing* 7 (1): 108–121.

Lundy, Brandon D. 2012. "The Involution of Democracy in Lusophone West Africa." In *Managing Conflicts in Africa's Democratic Transitions,* edited by Akanmu G. Adebayo, 119–140, 191. Lanham, MD: Lexington Books.

Marcelino, Pedro F. 2011. *The New Migration Paradigm of Transitional African Spaces: Inclusion, Exclusion, Liminality and Economic Competition in Transit Countries; A Case Study on the Cape Verde Islands.* Saarbrücken, Germany: Lambert Academic Publishing.

Marcelino, Pedro F. 2016. "The African 'Other' in the Cape Verde Islands: Interaction, Integration and the Forging of an Immigration Policy." In *The Upper Guinea Coast in Global Perspective*, edited by Jacqueline Knörr and Christoph Kohl, 116–134. New York: Berghahn Books.

Pardue, Derek. 2016. "'Cash or Body': Lessons on Space and Language from Cape Verdean Rappers and Their Beefs." *Popular Music and Society* 39 (3): 332–345.

Valdigem, A. 2010. "Boavista get to the streets for peace after a brutal murder. *GuinGuinBali: All About Africa*, October 5. http://www.guinguinbali.com/index.php?lang=enandmod=newsandtask=view_newsandcat=2andid=363.

Varela, Odair Barros, and Carlos Elias Barbosa. 2014. "Migration in Cape Verde Islands Legal and Policy Framework." *European Scientific Journal* (May Special Edition, ISSN: 1857-7881): 449–466.

World Bank Group. 2017. "Net Migration—Cabo Verde." World Bank, accessed September 18, 2017. http://data.worldbank.org/indicator/SM.POP.NETM?end=2012&locations=CV&start=2006&year_low_desc=false.

CHAPTER 5

Through a Glass Darkly

Kathleen B. Ingersoll and Daniel W. Ingersoll

Introduction

All peoples, societies, cultures, and individuals—even anthropologists—exhibit ethnocentrism at some level. One of the goals of anthropology is to overcome ethnocentrism—to escape cultural gnosticism, absolutism, and prejudice, and, ideally, to come as close to understanding the "mysterious other" as possible.

Function

Looking at culture as if it were a mechanism, that is from a functionalist perspective, a series of organizational categories are framed, in part deriving from how we see our own culture as a system of inter-related categories. If we look at familiar ethnographies (Firth 1957; Heider 1979; Hoebel 1960; Lowie 1956; Warner 1958), we observe the ethnographers presenting information in familiar categories such as religion, kinship, technology, politics, economy, warfare, rites and festivals, magic and medicine, and art. We have made the case elsewhere (Ingersoll 1989; Ingersoll and Nickell 1987) that American culture, and more broadly Western culture, is a categorical culture. The categories are part and parcel of how we perceive the world; we "think" in them and relate to them materially. Examples include the American three-part government system with its thousands of government agencies, occupations, academic disciplines (economics, political science, anthropology . . .), ranks, statuses, and scientific naming systems (biological taxonomy such as the Linnaean system;

the periodic charts, chemical names, etc.). In terms of material culture, we experience our Western world in dominantly rectilinear terms (like boxes, categories), both cognitively and materially, such as map coordinates, window and door panels, house rooms, storage spaces (bureaus, cabinets, post office mailboxes), framed art, game boards, city grids and rural farm sections, college land grants, and computer chips. It is not surprising that we might project our categorical imperatives onto other cultures. The risk—introducing distortion and misunderstanding.

As an illustration, suppose we Westerners, including anthropologists, view a Navajo sandpainting. We are inclined to interpret the "painting" in terms of our own system of cultural categories: art. As we wrote elsewhere:

> We watch in horror as the paintings are erased at the end of a curing ceremony. Even the anthropologist is barred from committing the sandpaintings to museums. Why is that? You need to put away the Western categories and take a holistic view of healing in Navajo culture to understand the drypaintings. Griffin-Pierce [1992, 55] wrote:

> "The sandpainting is considered to be a sacred living entity. The Anglo perception of a sandpainting as an artistic achievement misses the true meaning of the sandpainting. The physical beauty of the depicted image is insignificant in comparison to the ceremonial accuracy and sacredness of the depicted forms. The emphasis of the sandpaintings is on process, the dynamic flow of action, and on its ability to summon power through the process of its creation and use." (Ingersoll and Ingersoll 2013, 27)

For us, art is a separable experiential category that emphasizes individual originality, creativity, and, occasionally, fame. At home, we frame it, special category that art is, and display it on the wall. For the Navajo, it is not about a special technology or art

> . . . but about the power of knowledge, thought, words, mythic symbols, and the efficacy of the ritual itself to restore harmony and balance to a person or group. As the ritual unfolds, the sandpainting grows in depth and morphs, helping to tell stories and to merge past and present. You could not really exhibit a sandpainting in a museum; the upper surface of the sandpainting is just the final surface of a three-dimensional being. If you can grasp this, then not classifying sandpaintings as art makes perfect sense. (Ingersoll and Ingersoll 2013: 27)

Art? Talk about ethnocentrism.

The Mega the Better

In the way of routine technological assessments and evolutionary rankings, we do not seem to be able to help ourselves when encountering the products of other cultures: the bigger the better. If asked to list wonders of the world, we Westerners point to the mega: megalithic marvels like Stonehenge, skyscrapers, pyramids, ornate tombs, massive walls crossing continents, and grandiose architecture. If the culture in question ceases to construct the monumental, we may accuse them of collapse, regardless of whatever genius that culture possesses or possessed concerning ideas, concepts, or even small-scale material culture. When anthropologist H. Russell Bernard polled Americans (United States) in Florida, on what they rank as the great accomplishments of science and social science, he found that they tend to conceptualize science as engineering and technology, identifying "life-saving drugs, computers, space exploration, and so on" (2012, 1). Almost none of his respondents mentioned constitutions, encyclopedias, relativity theory, actuarial tables, time-motion studies, probability theory—ideas that have transformed the world and that made the technology possible. So, think of a sun circle a meter in diameter with little sticks assisting in the identical mental operations as at a Stonehenge—would we take notice? American cultural "marking" of "success" clearly gravitates toward the material, the physical, and the palpable (Bernard 2010) and, of course, the monumental. Ideas find themselves relegated to the dubious realm of the Ivory Tower (Bernard also quoted in Ingersoll and Ingersoll 2013, 24).

A case in point is Rapa Nui, where we have been doing research for a decade (see Figure 1).

FIGURE 1. Ahu Tongariki, Rapa Nui (photo by the authors).

Much of the Western world is enthralled by the giant *moai* on Rapa Nui, including anthropologists and archaeologists. When the Rapa Nui ceased to make *moai*, the Western world theorized collapse, catastrophe, ecocide, warfare, cannibalism . . . a veritable behavioral sink. Blinded by "megalomania," scholars nearly missed what was actually evolving culturally—changes comparable to what happened in the Western world at about the same time. When reviewing the Western world entry into that massive sea change from feudalism to capitalism, from monarchy to constitutional government, from ascribed to achieved status, from peasant horticulture to industrial agriculture, from craft to factory production, from castles to McMansions, what scholars proclaim "collapse!" (although maybe they should)? On Rapa Nui, in many ways, the shifts were from ascribed to achieved status (the Birdman competition), from a received landscape to a totally and highly productive and visibly transformed

FIGURE 2. Boulder gardens, Rapa Nui (photo by the authors).

landscape, from an isolated Pacific island into one in contact with all the oceans (trade with explorers, whalers, sealers), from *moai*-topped *ahu* to semi-pyramidal, sometimes containing *moai* as fill, and ship-shaped *ahu* (*ahu poe poe*) thought to imitate Western ships. The fixation on the *moai*—the Western "megalomania"—was so intense that it took observers of European derivation almost 300 years to understand that all those billions of rocks littering the landscape were not natural volcanic distributions, but humanly engineered and sustainable gardens as cultural as Arlington's stony cemeteries (see Figures 2 and 3).

Talk about ethnocentrism.

FIGURE 3. Two cultures intersecting, Oteo, Rapa Nui (photo by the authors).

Nature/Culture

One of Lévi-Strauss's structuralist axioms, implied or asserted, is that the nature/culture dichotomy is universal. Transformations occurring along a number of lines, featuring oppositions such as raw/cooked and male/female, operate in a dialectical fashion to transform nature into culture. Other social scientists joined in the discussion like Leach, Needham, and Ortner, and that discussion is still going on (see Malviya 2013; Papić 2017; Szpotowicz 2015). We certainly agree that the nature/culture dichotomy figures prominently in Western culture, as does a dialectical thought process that continuously transforms the culture and material culture of the

Western world. In a Weberian sense, we can trace the development of the symbols and their dialectical structures from Judeo-Christian prototypes in religion through their secularization to the present. The matter/spirit dichotomy appears in the first Genesis story as Yahweh systematically creates an entire cosmos of light, sky, water, land, plants, sun and stars, sea creatures, land animals, and, at the end, man. This is the realm of physical matter, emerging in a dialectic of oppositions such as separating light from darkness. Then in the second story of Genesis, the episodic order is somewhat altered, and man is created, then woman from man. Yahweh breaths spirit into dust, Adam and Eve consume the forbidden fruit, and the human cultural adventure begins as the first man and first woman are expelled from Eden to engage in their own creations: descendants, kinship, food, shelter, crime, war, cities, temples, kingdoms, and nations. The first story of Genesis is about matter and the second about spirit, creating a matter/spirit duality and dialectic. The matter/spirit dichotomy moves from there, to merge with concepts from Greek and Roman culture, and then out into the Western world as we know it. Table 1 illustrates some of the more prominent dual structures of the Western ethnographic present that can be traced back to the first two stories of Genesis (Genesis 1–2:4 and Genesis 2:4–22).

TABLE 1: Dual Structures
Genesis I / Genesis II
Matter / Spirit
Body / Soul or Spirit
Body / Mind
Nature / Culture
Nature / Nurture
History / Myth
Blood / In-Law
Physical / Mental
Reality / Myth

The continuously evolving dialectic, in both dual and trial variants, is present in the Christian Trinity, in the Cartesian mind/body dichotomy, in Hegel's and Marx's dialectical triads, in American governmental structure, in medical practice, and even in Western kinship blood vs. in-law relations (Schneider 1968, 1977) and the architecture of houses (Deetz 1977; Glassie 1975) (see Table 2 below). Anthropologist Lucy Garretson devotes a major portion of her book *American Culture* (1976) to examples of this nature/culture dialectic. A series of figures employing flow charts and boxes illustrates her analysis. In Garretson's Figure 1.1 (1976, 4), "The Role of the Constitution": "Nature | Transformed by | Human Rationality | Results in culture" exists parallel to "Anarchy | Transformed by | Law: U.S. Constitution | Results in | Government: Democracy." Her Figure 1.2 (1976, 7), "Transformation of the Wilderness," shows "Nature | Transformed by | Human Rationality | Results in Culture" in parallel with "Wilderness | Transformed by | Science and Technology | Results in | Abundance. Similarly, Figure 2.2 (1976, 17), "Love and Marriage," has "Nature | Transformed by | Rationality | Results in Culture" related in parallel to "Animal sexuality | Transformed by | Law: Marriage | Results in Nuclear family."

David Schneider's volume, *American Kinship* (1968), provided a source cited by Garretson, with his similar nature/reason/culture relational concept. Although not an exploration of dialectical structures *per se*, Alan Dundes, in "The Number Three in American Culture" (1980), furnishes hundreds of examples of the utilization of the number *three*.

While Western dualisms such as mind/body show opposition but no apparent movement, Western dialectic in its trinal mode is dynamic rather than static. It moves through oppositions, such as thesis encountering antithesis resulting in synthesis. The Garretson examples above illustrate this process.

TABLE 2: Trinal Structures

Trinity: Father/Son/Holy Ghost or Spirit
Hegelian-influenced (Fichte and others):
    Thesis/Antithesis/Synthesis,
    Being/Nothing/Becoming
Other examples include Freud, Id/Ego/Superego;
Garretson (1976), Nature/Human, Rationality/Culture;
and Schneider (1968, 108), Nature/Reason/Culture.

While some still subscribe to a universal nature/culture dichotomy, we think other ethnographers have managed to see beyond projections of our own dialectic. As examples, we would cite Claire Farrer's *Living Life's Circle: Mescalero Apache Cosmovision* (1991), Ann Fienup-Riordan's *Eskimo Essays: Yup'ik Lives and How We See Them* (1990), Mark Mosko's "The Symbols of 'Forest'" (1987), and Gary Witherspoon's *Language and Art in the Navajo Universe* (1977; also see Witherspoon 1975). What each of these ethnographies explores is the symbol systems central to these societies without reducing them to a dialectic about nature and culture. Mosko, beginning with the largely materialist and empirical literature contributed by Turnbull and others, shows that the Epulu Mbuti do not lack kinship but simply express relationships in a symbolic way not immediately recognizable to Westerners; here the previous researchers were not particularly interested in symbolic representations. He sketches their way of envisioning the world as a series of spheres and wombs (for a schematic representation, see Mosko 1987, p. 901, Figure 1). The contradiction involved, Mosko argues, is about endogamy versus exogamy. We would add it is clearly not about nature versus culture.

Claire Farrer in *Living Life's Circle* describes the "base metaphor" of the Mescalero Apache, which concerns harmony and balance tied to directionality, not nature versus culture (see Farrer 1991, p. 30,

Fig. 2.1, for a schematic representation). Furthermore, for Westerners, the matter of directionality needs to be considered *without* thinking about magnetic compasses and latitude and longitude—but rather how they, the Mescalero Apache, conceptualize the sun's movement.

Similarly, Ann Fienup-Riordan and Gary Witherspoon provide descriptions of core symbolic representations for the Yup'ik and Navajo, respectively—representations not at all about nature versus culture (see Witherspoon 1977, 33).

We suggest that until the equivalents of the "base metaphor" are recognized in any given culture besides our own, we have useful and valuable information but do not really achieve much of an understanding of that culture. We think this is the hardest gravity belt of all to escape. Required are years of exposure to another culture's thought world and the willingness to be bumped out of your footprints. Furthermore, our recognition as anthropologists probably requires mentoring from members of that culture who are deeply aware of their own symbolic and metaphoric constructions and can help us along.

Space and Time

We Westerners are definitely situated on the map: with longitude and latitude, compasses, transits, theodolites, loran, radar, satellites, and Google Earth. We Westerners are suspended between Creation and Apocalypse. That creation may be secular as in the Big Bang Theory, or it may reference the first two Genesis narratives. The end may be secular cosmic as in the sun becomes a black hole or theological Apocalypse as in Revelations. Either way, it is difficult for us to see things differently.

Regarding space, we will give just one illustration: an archaeological one. Imagine the construction of a Southeastern burial mound taking place over several years. Now imagine the archaeologists approaching the task of excavation. Should the mound be excavated by metrical levels or cultural and natural strata? The mound would have gradually grown, built by basket loads of earth being deposited in an ever-expanding form. An excavation by strata following the accumulation patterns will appear uneven, irregular, and perhaps even unscientific. Instead of following strata, the excavation could employ nice, even metrical levels, with precise intervals set as centimeters or inches or feet. The metrical levels look very orderly and scientific in the plans and profile views, but it becomes much more difficult to keep track of the original building pattern that way.

Regarding time, recall typical archaeological and cultural divisions, often three-part: Early, Middle, Late; Paleolithic, Mesolithic, Neolithic; Savagery, Barbarism, Civilization (Morgan); magic, religion, science (Frazer); separation, transition, incorporation (Van

FIGURE 4. Photograph of a poster for the film *Rapa Nui*, Hanga Roa, Rapa Nui (photo by the authors).

Gennep), etc. We project our ideas of development and evolution into our parsing of our data. How much do these counter the lived experience of the cultures or societies that we attempt to study?

Now we will return to Rapa Nui for our final illustration. Above, we discussed cultural collapse as a label applied when an advanced (in our estimation) culture ceases to construct the monumental. Of course, the collapse could also relate to the apparent failure of a political, economic, or food production system. What happened to the Maya, the Anasazi, the Romans, the Medieval Norse on Greenland, to Ancient Mesopotamian societies? Why did they collapse? Well, not all accept collapse at face value—for example, see McAnany and Yoffee (2010).

There's a whole realm of apocalyptic stuff out there in the form of comics, novels, films, and science predictions—for instance, see the films *Apocalypse Now* or *Melancholia*. In the film *Rapa Nui*, the end of the *moai* world is prophesied, as the last palm tree is felled. Now no more *moai* can be moved; now no more canoes can be built; now no one can leave the island or fish the oceans; now the kinship groups engage in warfare (Figure 4). Apocalyptic scenarios like this tell more about us than them. It is our projection of Biblical creation through Revelations drama, and its secular transforms onto mysterious *other*.

Talk about ethnocentrism.

Introspection and Ecstasis

Introspection and ecstasis are two ways of approaching cultural analysis. Introspection involves looking into one's mental, emotional, or philosophical self. We think this is an appropriate approach to analysis in psychology, psychiatry, and philosophy within our own Western cultural sphere. But we do not think introspection works well when applied to non-Western cultures: the risk is projection of our Western culture, selves, and minds onto others. We look inward, then discover our categories, concepts, values, behaviors, and symbols where they may not actually find expression—as with the example of Navajo "sandpaintings" as art, above. Sociologist Peter Berger comments on introspection:

> Since society is encountered by the individual as a reality external to himself, it may often happen that its workings remain opaque to his understanding. He cannot discover the meaning of a social phenomenon by introspection. He must, for this purpose, go outside himself and engage in the basically same kind of empirical inquiry that is necessary if he is to understand anything located outside his own mind. (1969, 11)

Instead, what we really need is to be bumped out of our footprints—to be able to see what's around us in a new way. In sociology (Berger 1969, 1973) and anthropology (Goulet and Miller 2007), the term ecstasy, from the Greek *ekstasis*, literally meaning "stepping" or "standing outside," is employed to reference this approach. While "ecstasy" tends to be used in the literature, we prefer to use the form "ecstasis" to indicate a special analytical term, distinguishing it from the everyday word "ecstasy," which has a wide range of meanings. Berger wrote:

> A useful concept to introduce in this connection is that of "ecstasy." By this we refer not to some abnormal heightening of consciousness in a mystic sense, but rather, quite literally, to the active standing or stepping outside (literally, *ekstasis*) the taken-for-granted routines of society. In our discussion of "alternation" we have already touched upon a very important form of "ecstasy" in our sense, namely, the one that takes place when an individual is enabled to jump from world to world in his social existence. However, even without such an exchange of

universes it is possible to achieve distance and detachment vis-à-vis one's own world. As soon as a given role is played without inner commitment, deliberately and deceptively, the actor is in an ecstatic state with regard to his "world-taken-for-granted." What others regard as fate, he looks upon as a set of factors to reckon with in his operations. What others assume to be essential identity, he handles as a convenient disguise. In other words, "ecstasy" transforms one's awareness of society in such a way that *givenness* becomes *possibility*. While this begins as a state of consciousness, it should be evident that sooner or later there are bound to be significant consequences in terms of action. From the point of view of the official guardians of order, it is dangerous to have too many individuals around playing the social game with inner reservations. (1973, 136–7; also see Berger 1969, 43)

Experiencing ecstasis can help us understand our own culture, as described by sociologist Berger, but especially so, perhaps, for other cultural conceptions of the world. How does this happen? In the edited volume *Extraordinary Anthropology*, Goulet and Miller describe the process in their Introduction (2007, 1–16). Goulet and Miller write:

In "Ethnographic Objectivity: From Rigor to Vigor," the opening chapter of *Anthropology with an Attitude: Critical Essays*, Fabian maintains that "much of our ethnographic research is carried out best when we are 'out of our minds,' that is, while we relax our inner controls, forget our purposes, let ourselves go. In short, there is an ecstatic side to fieldwork which should be counted among the conditions of knowledge production, hence of objectivity." (Fabian 2001, 31 cited in Goulet and Miller 2007, 1).

Goulet and Miller follow with additional reference to Fabian:

> It is in this vein that we explore the contents, preconditions, and ethnographic relevance of the "ecstatic side of fieldwork"—including, but not exclusively, experiences of personality and socially significant visions or dreams in the context of fieldwork. From this vantage point, "ecstasis, like empathy, communication, and dialog, as well as age, gender, social class, and relations of power, belongs to concepts that impose themselves when we reflect critically about what makes us succeed or fail in our efforts to produce knowledge about Others" as we interact with them in their worlds. (Fabian 2000, 280 cited in Goulet and Miller 2007, 3–4)

Many of the contributors to the Goulet and Miller volume in their chapters describe the impact of participation in ritual, dance, apprenticeship, and other forms of experiential participation: not just observing but also taking part. For example, in the chapter by Meintel (2007, 149, 151, 155) Edith Turner's work was cited, ranging from Edith's participation in healing events and rituals with the Ndembu (1992) and Alaskans, the sense of *communitas* that she and Victor felt in their work, and their own embracing of Catholicism helping them to fathom the healing rituals of others.

But intense, ecstatic emotional experience is not the only avenue to understanding. Below, we give examples of how we felt we experienced ecstasis through the contributions of others. One of the first world view breakthroughs one of us attained (Daniel) was through the ethnography of Gary Witherspoon (1975, 1977). After years of reading numerous ethnographies about the Navajo, all that information, while useful, just seemed two-dimensional; but when reading Witherspoon, the whole Navajo thought world came alive for the first time, everything from basic symbols (SNBH) to language and narrative, and all those other ethnographies came into focus.

Maybe part of his edge came from marriage to a Navajo woman—as I recall about fifteen years or so at the time of writing the sources cited above. There's something to be said about learning from a long-term teacher. An amusing quote illustrates one of Gary Witherspoon's own insights while he was exploring Navajo syntax, in this case, of a phrase generated by an experiment in transformational grammar—a phrase seemingly grammatically correct but culturally discordant. Witherspoon wrote:

> Taking a cultural approach to the explanation of this pattern in Navajo syntax, some years ago I asked my wife why it was so absurd to say *tó at'ééd boodláá'* 'the water was drunk by the girl'. She thought long and hard about this matter, unable to see why it was not absurd to me. Finally, she said, "The sentence attributes more intelligence to the water than it does to the girl, and anyone [even you was the implication] ought to know that human beings are smarter than water." Therein I had a lead to solve this riddle, but I was not sure what to make of it. She went on to say that the water does not think, so how could it have the girl drink it. But, I insisted, the water was not acting or thinking, it just got drunk. She countered by saying that the way I had constructed that sentence made it appear that the water was the cause of the drinking action, not the girl.
>
> From the discussion above I later surmised that maybe the sentence should be translated 'the water caused the girl to drink it'. I tried this translation out on several Navajos who knew English. They said it was much closer to the Navajo meaning of the sentence than 'the water was drunk by the girl' but they were still a little uncomfortable with it. After some further thought and discussion, we came up with the translation 'the water let the girl

drink it'. Therein we had captured in English not just the covert meaning of the Navajo sentence but the overt absurdity that the meaning expressed. (1977, 67; brackets in the original)

If you have ever played the game of Mad Libs, you can get the sense of how this works in English.

Gary Witherspoon benefitted from working closely with a number of Navajo, but also or especially his wife. Claire Farrer, author of *Living Life's Circle: Mescalero Apache Cosmovision*, benefitted from working closely with someone: "Bernard Second was my mentor and the one to whom I owe the primary debt of gratitude. As will be apparent, there would be no book without him; truly this book is as much his as mine. As the earlier epigraph indicates, this book was important to him. My regret is he did not live to see its publication" (1991, xi). Working with Bernard Second, she was able to become aware of what she called the base metaphor, a symbol structure that provides a powerful key to bringing Mescalero Apache ethnography to life.

After reading Eskimo-Inuit-Yup'ik ethnography for years but still not really understanding Eskimo tales or rituals, in this case first insights came from an archaeological report by Robert McGhee (1977), who began wondering why some Thule (about 1000–1600 AD, Alaska to Labrador and Greenland) artifacts he was studying in museum collections tended to be made of antler (caribou) while others tended to be made from sea ivory or sea mammal bone. The distributions could not be resolved by functional characteristics of the materials—either would be satisfactory for any of the artifacts. Having read structuralists like Leach (1973), he began perusing the historic and ethnographic literature on Eskimo myth, religion, taboos, etc. What he discovered was a series of related pairings (we hesitate to use the term "oppositions" because the concepts are not related in a dialectical or adversarial fashion—it is more like the pairing for us of, say, salt and pepper, and we pass them together at the table):

Male	Female
Land	Sea
Summer	Winter
Caribou	Sea mammals, sea birds
antler	ivory

Now the materials associated with the artifact made sense; so did the stories like "Sedna and the Fulmar" from one end of the arctic to the other; so did many of the once odd taboos (to Westerners). It all began with McGhee's analysis of material culture. The work of Fienup-Riordan (1990) similarly provides a means to a new understanding of the contemporary Yup'ik thought and culture: everything come magically into focus.

Writers like Basso, Farrer, Fienup-Riordan, Griffin-Pierce, Mc-Ghee, Mosko, and Witherspoon have helped us to step out of our own ethnocentric footprints, to see relationships within a culture not seen before, to then be able to integrate the varied ethnographic perspectives on a single culture. And then, coming back to our own culture with new tools, we can see our own dialectical existence—of which so much resides at an unconscious level—more clearly, and realize that it is not universal as Lévi-Strauss imagined the nature/culture duality to be.

We conclude, in the way of suggesting effective antidotes to ethnocentrism: of course, being there, in another place, as in conducting fieldwork, is hard to beat; direct participation in another's emotionally charged world like ritual, dance, or music; and if you cannot get out the door, drawing on the experience and insights of others like anthropologists who have been there. We/you will never be able to totally escape the condition of ethnocentrism—

even as anthropologists—but we can devote ourselves to treating the symptoms.

This chapter is based on our paper, "Through a Glass Darkly," presented at the 52nd Annual Meeting of the Southern Anthropological Society, in the session "In and Out of the Classroom: Engaging Student Learners with Issues of Ethnocentrism," March 25, 2017. Our thanks to Marjorie Snipes.

Bibliography

Apocalypse Now. 1979. Film produced, directed, and co-written by Francis Ford Coppola. Co-written by John Milius. Distributed by United Artists.

Basso, Keith H. 1996. *Wisdom Sits in Places: Landscape and Language Among the Western Apache.* Albuquerque: University of New Mexico Press.

Berger, Peter L. (1967) 1969. *The Sacred Canopy: Elements of a Sociological Theory of Religion.* New York: Anchor Press.

Berger, Peter L. 1973. *Invitation to Sociology: A Humanistic Perspective.* Woodstock, NY: Overlook Press.

Bernard, H. Russell. 2010. "The Secret Life of Social Science." Lecture delivered at St. Mary's College of Maryland, Department of Anthropology, Distinguished Scholar Program, February 15, 2010.

Bernard, H. Russell. 2012. "The Science in Social Science." *PNAS Early Edition* (United States of America). http://www.pnas.org/content/early/2012/11/29/1218054109, 1–4.

Deetz, James. 1977. *In Small Things Forgotten.* Garden City, NY: Anchor Books.

Dundes, A. 1980. "The Number Three in American Culture." In *Interpreting Folklore*, 134–159. Bloomington: Indiana University Press.

Fabian, Johannes. 2000. *Out of Our Minds: Reason and Madness in the Exploration of Central Africa.* Berkeley: University of California Press.

Fabian, Johannes. 2001. *Anthropology with an Attitude: Critical Essays.* Stanford: Stanford University Press.

Farrer, Claire. 1991. *Living Life's Circle: Mescalero Apache Cosmovision.* Albuquerque: University of New Mexico Press.

Fienup-Riordan, Ann. 1990. *Eskimo Essays: Yup'ik Lives and How We See Them.* New Brunswick: Rutgers University Press.

Firth, Raymond. (1936) 1957. *We, the Tikopia: Kinship in Primitive Polynesia.* Boston: Beacon Press.

Frazer, James George. (1911) 1966. *The Golden Bough: A Study in Magic and Religion.* New York: St. Martin's Press.

Garretson, Lucy R. 1976. *American Culture: An Anthropological Perspective.* Dubuque, IA: Wm. C. Brown.

Glassie, Henry. 1975. *Folk Housing in Middle Virginia.* Knoxville: University of Tennessee Press.

Goulet, Jean-Guy, and Bruce Granville Miller, eds. 2007. *Extraordinary Anthropology: Transformations in the Field.* Lincoln: University of Nebraska Press.

Griffin-Pierce, Trudy. 1992. *Earth is My Mother, Sky is My Father: Space, Time, and Astronomy in Navajo Sandpainting.* Albuquerque: University of New Mexico Press.

Heider, Karl. 1979. *Grand Valley Dani: Peaceful Warriors.* New York: Holt, Rinehart and Winston.

Hoebel, E. Adamson. 1960. *The Cheyennes: Indians of the Great Plains.* New York: Holt, Rinehart and Winston.

Ingersoll, Daniel W. Jr. "American House Archetypes." Paper delivered at the Society for Historical Archaeology, Conference on Historical and Underwater Archaeology, January 10, 1989.

Ingersoll, Daniel W. Jr., and Kathleen Butler Ingersoll. 2013. "Art as Distraction: Rocking the Farm." In *The Art of Anthropology/The Anthropology of Art*, edited by Brandon D. Lundy, 23–64. Knoxville, TN: Newfound Press.

Ingersoll, Daniel W. Jr., and James M. Nickell. 1987. "The Most Important Monument: The Tomb of the Unknown Soldier." In *Mirror and Metaphor: Material and Social Constructions of Reality*, edited by D. W. Ingersoll and G. Bronitsky, 199–225. Lanham, MD: University Press of America.

Leach, E. 1970. *Claude Lévi-Strauss.* New York: Viking.

Leach, Edmund. 1973. "Concluding Address." In *The Explanation of Culture Change,* edited by Colin Renfrow, 761–771. Pittsburgh: University of Pittsburgh Press.

Lévi-Strauss, Claude. 1967. *Structural Anthropology*. Vol. 1. Translated from the French by Claire Jacobsen and Brooke Grundfest Schoepf. Garden City, NY: Doubleday.

Lévi-Strauss, Claude. 1975. *The Raw and the Cooked. Introduction to a Science of Mythology*, Vol. 1. New York: Harper Colophon.

Lévi-Strauss, Claude. 1976. *Structural Anthropology*, Vol. 2. Translated from the French by Monique Layton. Chicago: University of Chicago Press.

Lowie, Robert H. (1935) 1956. *The Crow Indians*. New York: Holt, Rinehart and Winston.

Malviya, Saumya. *2013*. "Claude Levi-Strauss and the Nature Culture Opposition." Dissertation submitted to the University of Delhi. http://www.academia.edu/28964416/CLAUDE_LÉVI_STRAUSS_AND_THE_NATURE_CULTURE_OPPOSITION.

McAnany, Patricia A., and Norman Yoffee, eds. 2010. *Questioning Collapse: Human Resilience, Ecological Vulnerability, and the Aftermath of Empire*. Cambridge: Cambridge University Press.

McGhee, Robert 1977. "Ivory for the Sea Woman: The Symbolic Attributes of a Prehistoric Technology." *Canadian Journal of Archaeology* 1: 141–149.

Meintel, Deidre. 2007. "When the Extraordinary Hits Home: Experiencing Spiritualism." In *Extraordinary Anthropology: Transformations in the Field*, edited by Jean-Guy Goulet and Bruce Granville Miller, 124–157. Lincoln: University of Nebraska Press.

Melancholia. 2011. Directed and written by Lars von Trier. Produced by Meta Louise Foldager and Louise Vesth. Distributed by Nordisk Film.

Morgan, Lewis H. 1909. *Ancient Society or Researches in the Lines of Human Progress from Savagery through Barbarism to Civilization*. Chicago: Charles H. Kerr.

Mosko, Mark S. 1987. "The Symbols of 'Forest': A Structural Analysis of Mbuti Culture and Social Organization." *American Anthropologist* 89 (4): 896–913.

Needham, Rodney. 1972. *Belief, Language, and Experience*. Chicago: University of Chicago Press.

Papić, Žarana. 2017. "The Opposition Between Nature and Culture as the 'Natural' Definition and Interpretation of Sexual Difference—Levi-Strauss' Projection of the Origins of Culture as a Social Contract Between Men." http://www.zenskestudie.edu.rs/en/publishing/online-material/women-s-studies-journal/292-the-opposition-between-nature-and-culture-as-the-natural-definition-and-interpretation-of-sexual-difference-levi-strauss-projection-of-the-origins-of-culture-as-a-social-contract-between-men.

Schneider, David M. 1968. *American Kinship: A Cultural Account.* Englewood Cliffs, NJ: Prentice-Hall.

Schneider, David M. 1977. "Kinship, Nationality, and Religion in American Culture: Toward a Definition of Kinship." In *Symbolic Anthropology: A Reader in the Study of Symbols and Meanings,* edited by Janet L. Dolgin, David S. Kremnitzer, and David M. Schneider, 63–71. New York: Columbia University Press.

Szpotowicz, Diana. 2015. "What's the Relationship between 'Nature' and 'Culture'?" http://www.linkedin.com/pulse/whats-relationship-between-nature-culture-diana-szpotowicz.

Turner, Edith, with William Blodgett, Singleton Kahona, and Benwa Fideli. 1992. *Experiencing Ritual: A New Interpretation of African Healing.* Philadelphia: University of Pennsylvania Press.

Van Gennep, Arnold. (1909) 1960. *The Rites of Passage.* Translated by Monika B. Vizedom and Gabrielle L. Caffee. Chicago: University of Chicago Press.

Warner, W. Lloyd. (1937) 1958. *A Black Civilization: A Study of an Australian Tribe.* New York: Harper and Row.

Witherspoon, Gary. 1975. *The Central Concepts of Navajo World View.* Lisse, Netherlands: Peter De Ridder Press. PdR Press Publications in World View 1.

Witherspoon, Gary. 1977. *Language and Art in the Navajo Universe.* Ann Arbor: University of Michigan Press.

CHAPTER 6

Feeding Variety: Challenging the Standard American Diet through Nutrition Education

Ayla Samli

Introduction

Although anthropologists, such as Mary Douglas (2003) and Sidney Mintz (1986), have looked into the ritual significance of food and food preparation over time and in great depth, the Standard American Diet has not been as compelling a subject of study, despite its sociocultural significance. Compared to feasts in Papua New Guinea and the whithertos and wherefores of pork proscriptions among the ancient Jews, the Standard American Diet (SAD) is a newer dietary creation, one that pervades everyday life, a mundane staple of nutrition in the United States. This paper will not investigate the Standard American Diet in detail. Instead, it will consider the features of nutrition interventions for school-aged children and adult refugees.

The paper's findings are drawn from observations and anecdotal data from Recipe for Success, a nutrition education program funded by a grant from the US Department of Agriculture's Supplemental Nutrition Assistance Program–Education (SNAP-Ed) and the North Carolina Department of Health and Human Services and housed in the Anthropology department of the University of North Carolina at Greensboro. Because my previous research focused on how gender functions in Istanbul households, this speculative project on nutrition in the United States is a departure from my expertise; so this paper is preliminary, theoretical, and reflexive. I recognize that the anthropology of food has a long history, and this paper will not address that in detail; however, it draws on my own humanistic orientation to culture. Coming to a new research topic from a different set of disciplinary questions entails looking awry at the field, reaping both the risks and benefits of naiveté and unconventionality. Different orientations keep our discipline dynamic. Like food sampling, I appreciate the opportunity to try something new and unfamiliar.

The Standard American Diet finds its origins in industrialization, which created a cascade of lifestyle changes for Americans participating in industrial labor, who began to rely on different modes of transport, work, and packaged foods. Wiedman (2012) details the health effects of industrialization on Native Americans beginning in the 1940s and throughout the subsequent decades. As working Native Americans adopted a SAD diet, they also suffered from its far-reaching health effects, including increased cholesterol, heart disease, and diabetes. But this diet not only impacts the bodies that consume it—the SAD also impacts consumption. In her book *Dangerous Digestion*, Melanie DePuis (2015) suggests that the Standard American Diet also informs cultural values surrounding food and food nutrition and that the embrace of the SAD results in the shutting down of other food options. She states: "Understanding S. A. D. also requires knowing the ways in which the cheap meat-centered diet stigmatized fiber-filled diets of other Americans—the greens and beans eating cultures of China, Mexico, and the black and white South" (100). So, the SAD, gaining status over local, traditional foods, has suppressed and overtaken nutritious, indigenous eating habits. Over time, SAD food has become more accessible and affordable than traditional foods.

The Standard American Diet exists within a whole culture of consuming cheap resources, as DuPuis details in the following statement: "Cheap food fits into a larger American bargain among industry (cheap wages), workers (cheap food), and the middle class (moral superiority), enabling each to fill a role and to gain advantages from that role" (2015, 99). Thus, the Standard American Diet functions within a political economy of labor and industry, making it much bigger than food. Food inequity relates to this political economic system, and it has been reinforced by the "food revolution" focused on healthful eating. Healthful food has become more expensive as cheaper food has become more widely available. DuPuis analyzes bifurcation of food access according to socioeconomic status. "As cheap food becomes even more industrialized and processed, the poor are eating more of it while those who have the means avoid it. The poor are then blamed for their faulty lifestyles, leading to new policies to control the consumption of those at fault" (DePuis 2015, 99). When nutritious foods are replaced with calorie-dense ones, the health effects are far reaching (Grotto and Zied 2010).

Although the impulse might be to consider SAD out in society through its many iterations in media and marketing, how the SAD is perpetuated through households where it might be challenged through nutritious alternatives deserves investigation. Perhaps a corollary to SAD is the category of whiteness—it is that unmarked, taken-for-granted category against which all others are measured. In the book *The Possessive Investment in Whiteness*, George Lipsitz identifies whiteness "as the unmarked category against which difference is constructed, whiteness never has to speak its name, never has to acknowledge its rule as an organizing principle in social and cultural relations" (2006, 1). The Standard American Diet sets the standard against which other diets are measured; it is comfort food and fast food, thus rendering vegetable-based diets less homey. As the place where comfort is created, home is, by nature, ethnocentric—because home meals come out of parents' eating habits and conceptions of food. If we want to combat the invisible hegemony, or the ethnocentrism, of the Standard American Diet we have to explore food outside of the home.

Many of us can think back on our childhood meals as a perpetuation of certain signature dishes, values, and tastes. My partner mentioned that one of his father's favorite dishes in rotation was Roman Holiday (which is basically homemade hamburger helper), while I remember many, many servings of turkey tetrazzini (a turkey and cheese casserole). These comfort foods did not make vegetables the focus. As a middle-class parent today, I have visited many US homes where children are offered separate meals of SAD food compared to their parents or older siblings—especially pasta or grilled cheese and chicken fingers. In the study "Eating Fruits and Vegetables: An Ethnographic Study of American and French Family Dinners," the authors note that working parents of both cultures who live busy lives certainly feed their children prepared foods and maintain control over how, when, and what they eat (Kremer-Sadlik et al. 2015). The authors suggest that their "observations also afford insights into parents' beliefs about what children should eat, and into parents' talk and behavior patterns that socialize children into certain eating habits . . ." (85). This quote reveals that mealtimes serve as opportunities for the inculcation of values, socialization of tastes, and a chance to perpetuate cultural norms and familial habits related to food. The ethnographic study, comparing American with French children's food sampling habits, shows that French children are offered a variety of vegetables at meal times, through courses, that they usually taste a bite, and that they are not provided with alternative foods. Although it might be appealing to tell Americans to simply emulate French dining habits for the sake of their children's future palettes and health, that is not happening; so what other kinds of eating environments can Americans create?

Nutrition Education for American Schoolchildren

Recipe for Success, operating out of UNC Greensboro's Anthropology department, offers nutrition education to SNAP-eligible populations, which includes some Title 1 schools. Although the explicit goal of Recipe for Success is to increase intake of fruits and vegetables, the goal depends on developing awareness of a diversity of fruits and vegetables, of nurturing a taste for them, and learning how they might be incorporated into daily life.

I will now present some vignettes and observations about the sampling environments that foster experimentation and openness to foods. Recipe for Success presents children with various opportunities for food sampling. Recipe for Success educators typically offer a lesson related to the food (such as the importance of eating colorful fruits and vegetables), followed by a food tasting. In smaller classes, children—who are usually elementary aged—are invited to help prepare the food that they sample. The following describes aspects of the sampling atmospheres, which might be useful in considering how to frame exploring unfamiliar foods.

1. *There's no place like home*

Recipe for Success uses libraries, schools, and community recreation centers for nutrition education, places that are clearly outside of the home. This "not-homeness" calls on different roles of engagement for children and food, allowing them to break with prejudices against foods. One example my former colleague Kimberly Titlebaum provided was when a little boy helped her to cut and prepare tuna salad with celery and apples. Although he had refused to eat tuna salad at home, he ate it during the food sampling, with some trepidation. This observation illustrates that eating outside of the home can be perceived as a threat to the order established by home life. The child's grandmother later claimed that he now prepares this special dish for his family on a regular basis. As a point of convergence, when I conducted research on domestic life in Turkey, many of the housewives I interviewed warned me against the perils of eating outside of the house in cafes or restaurants, because it might be dangerous and I would not know who was cooking the food. These warnings struck me as indicators of how highly threatening (and potentially promising) dining out might be in terms of disrupting the norms (both gender and food related) of home. Although grabbing a bite to eat elsewhere is customary in American society, I submit that it can also offer a dangerous, transgressive opportunity for children to sample and expand their palettes. For American children, taking risks with new foods might be easier outside of the home than within the home itself.

2. *The Tone of Exploration*

In the school classrooms I have visited, food sampling is met with openness and curiosity—perhaps because classroom teacher and nutrition educators have also set up a standard of behavior where all students try all of the foods offered. Setting up the sampling as an expected behavior allows all of the children to try the foods as a group. This could perhaps be explained through a Goffman-esque analysis of students' acting in their perceived roles, which in this case is to try new food. As an obligation and a learning expectation, food sampling becomes part of the students' responsibility in fulfilling their expected roles. When trying new foods functions as part of a student's daily work, the task shifts how the student perceives the experience of sampling. Students do not often have the luxury of turning down teachers' assignments, so food tasting becomes another assignment for the day. In some of the classrooms I visited the students met these new foods with excitement and enthusiasm.

3. *Transgressive Treats*

Many of the foods children have sampled in my presence transgress their everyday norms and expectations of foods. For example, in a class on fruit and vegetable subgroups, we gave students kale chips. Additionally, red and yellow bell peppers cut into scoops to dip hummus and guacamole serve as crunchy alternatives to potato chips. A number of children dispensed with dipping the sample spread and begged for more peppers. Again, the form of the food—serving as a dipper instead of on a salad or stuffed—might hold more interest for students who might have encountered it in different contexts. In these samplings, vegetables take on the leading roles and are met with enthusiasm. All of these foods are presented in a defamiliarized manner, out of the home context and often using textures and flavors that are either unfamiliar or defamiliarized to the students. Victor Shklovsky discussed the defamiliarization of words through poetry: "The purpose of art is to impart the sensation of things as they are perceived and not as they are known. The technique of art is to make objects 'unfamiliar,' to make forms difficult, to increase the difficulty and length of perception because the process of perception is an aesthetic end in itself and must be prolonged" (Shklovsky 2016, 16). Similar to poetry that presents words in new contexts—foods, in these sampling contexts, standing alone or in concert with other foods in an unconventional manner, make foods stand out and remove them from their familiar stereotypes. This experience of foods creates the opportunity for new tastes, new perceptions.

4. *Diversity: Eating Rainbows*

At the public schools where Recipe for Success provides nutrition classes, the classrooms themselves are culturally diverse, so students sometimes bring into the class their own experiences with foods, serving as ambassadors to some of the food sampled. Guacamole, succotash, or beets might be staples in some households and completely foreign in others. However, in an environment that encourages exploration and some excitement, students can bring their familiarity with foods to the communal table. Students growing up on farms, for example, sometimes recognize succotash as a summer staple at home, while some students bring their familiarity with hummus to the classroom table. Leveraging students' own diverse food tastes to promote tastings helps to leverage the diversity within the classroom. At the end of the day, commensality, the act of sharing food together, experiencing exciting and diverse flavors among children who come from diverse backgrounds, helps to do the work to create nutrition awareness—and awareness of one another. Diverse food is critical for fighting nutritional deficiencies brought on by SAD—and for fighting ethnocentrism.

Thinking Diversely: When the Standard American Diet is Not the Standard

During the summer of 2017, Maurine Crouch (a former colleague from Recipe for Success and current Master's candidate in Public Health) and I developed a collaboration with a local nonprofit that serves newly arrived refugees, including adults and children, from several war-torn areas. The barriers to providing these adults with nutrition education were significant: their English was limited; their dietary habits and customs were very diverse; and navigating federal assistance programs such as the Special Supplemental Nutrition Program for Women, Infants, and Children (WIC) and the Supplemental Nutrition Assistance Program (SNAP) was unfamiliar.

Culturally Inflected Challenges to Nutrition Education
Attempting to develop nutrition education for these underserved populations was quite challenging. Drawing on the resources avail-

able through SNAP-Ed, my colleagues and I conducted a lesson regarding reading nutrition labels. Through translators, various refugee groups investigated the sugar and salt content of different foods, including potato chips and sugary carbonated drinks. In addition to working on food literacy, we conducted a tasting of WIC-eligible foods. These tastings included several cereals, dairy milk, and milk alternatives. Because cereal is one of the foods available through WIC but not necessarily a staple for different populations, tastings allowed the refugees to encounter these foods and see their varied uses. Cereal can be served with milk, eaten dry as a snack, or even used as breading on other foods. Helping the refugees to both sample and consider the possibilities of the foods might make the foods more useable.

In terms of dairy milk, the director of the institute emphasized to me that dairy milk is a problem for many Asian refugee groups. Not only is it not a standard beverage for their diets but there is evidence that Asians tend to be more lactose intolerant than other populations (Swagerty et al. 2002). Dairy milk alternatives are available through WIC, so the Recipe for Success workers conducted tastings of soymilk and cow's milk, with and without cereal. These tastings presented refugees with alternatives to their familiar breakfasts but also presented these alternatives in different use contexts. Cereals could be mixed with nuts and eaten dry or served with yogurt for lunch. In other words, expecting them to assimilate American eating habits was not viable, but helping them to consider how to incorporate these available foods seemed to be a more persuasive approach. The director of the program stated that refugees needed assistance navigating WIC and SNAP, learning which foods were and were not eligible, and incorporating those foods into their habits. However, my observations suggest that the supplemental nutrition programs themselves are limited and ethnocentric.

If certain populations traditionally eat white rice for three meals a day, for example, then the allocations of cereal (presumably breakfast), whole grain bread (presumably lunch), and brown rice (dinner) do not meet the needs of those populations. It may be reasonable to help them to taste brown rice as an alternative to white rice; however, the guidelines for how much and what may be bought using WIC assumes that several grains are being eaten during different mealtimes.

In terms of dairy, if certain populations are lactose intolerant or do not consume cereal with milk, cheese, or yogurts, then the allocations of both dairy and cereals do not take into consideration the habits and limitations of those ethnic groups. Sampling dairy alternatives provides the refugees with the opportunity to encounter the foods available to them; however, incorporating those foods into a daily routine may be a long process. Whether the provided alternatives are healthier than the indigenous foods being replaced warrants further investigation.

As a cultural anthropologist who was working as a nutrition educator, I felt a disconnect between my job and my deeply-held ethical commitments. I wanted the refugees to eat and to succeed in North American society, but I was not convinced that the foods they were being allocated were healthier than the foods to which they were accustomed. In order to benefit from SNAP and WIC, refugees would have to assimilate to what was effectively a SAD breakfast and lunch. Helping them to navigate their limited choices was one form of help I could offer. However, I see the effects of SAD assimilation in my own family.

A First-Generation American Considers the SAD Reality
My father, an immigrant from Turkey, has told me, many times, the story of his arrival in the United States. When he arrived in the 1950s as an immigrant, his funds were very limited. He was able to afford

one meal a day, and so he subsisted on one hamburger and a mug of warm milk and honey. To give up a cuisine of fresh fruit and vegetables at every meal to embrace one of processed food as his entire day's diet was necessary for his survival. This transition was also a part of his assimilation to the United States; he embraced the language, the food, and the orientation to work. He thrived professionally, and his health suffered from all of the poor outcomes precipitated by the SAD he embraced.

However, there is more plurality and more recognition of diversity in the United States today, and immigrants bring with them valued knowledge about their culinary traditions. The diet he left behind, the Mediterranean diet, is currently ranked as the number one best diet by *U.S. News and World Report* (2018) for its diabetes and cancer prevention capabilities. As the child of an immigrant, I connect with the flavors and traditions of my father's homeland and consider it part of my inheritance. I have had the privilege of studying the culture my father left behind, learning to cook the foods of my heritage by sneaking into the kitchen of an Istanbul restaurant and visiting my Turkish family still living there. I hope that newly arrived refugees and immigrants will have the opportunity to experience, recreate, and remember their families' foods. If they are subsisting solely on WIC-provided resources, they will have to give up many of those traditions until they find the monetary and culinary resources to once again eat their cultural foods.

Feeding the Future

During the summer, the nonprofit institute provided an array of programmed activities for the refugees' children who were out of school. These children ranged in age from about five to sixteen, and their English fluency varied immensely. As the parents took

English classes, my Recipe for Success colleagues and I organized many of the same activities for the refugee children that we usually present to schoolchildren in local Title 1 schools. However, because the refugee students lack the English proficiency to perform the activities, the exercises served the dual purpose of talking about nutrition and teaching English. We brainstormed "rainbows of foods," locating green and red fruits and vegetables. I heard "avocado" over and over, enthusiastically, because it was an already familiar and favored food. Unlike the Title 1 English-speaking schoolchildren we usually encountered, the children of refugees and immigrants had more prior knowledge of fruits and vegetables; however, some of the local vegetables and fruits were not as familiar or looked different from their native ones. Strawberries, for example, were a new summer favorite. As my colleagues and I worked to provide sampling opportunities of different kinds of foods while developing the vocabularies of tastes—adding salt and sugar to oranges, for example, to highlight the words *sweet* and *salty*—learning was happening. The children were developing an appreciation of different foods in different contexts, learning the lexicon of words associated with fruits and vegetables, practicing English with one another, and developing confidence as speakers. However, the refugee children were also being indoctrinated into a diet more easily supported by the resources available to their newly-arrived families.

I can imagine nutrition classes where newly arrived refugees and immigrants participate alongside of their Title 1 counterparts to explore, sample, and enjoy exciting and healthy flavors and possibilities from an array of cultural backgrounds. Traditional diets are developing a greater presence in nutrition education. Resources such as Oldways (http://oldwayspt.org/traditional-diets) introduce several culturally-inflected diets to everyday audiences. Because the health, environmental, and cultural costs of suppressing indigenous diets are so pronounced, now is a good time to cultivate even more awareness of alternatives to the Standard American Diet. Those alternative foods also need to be made more available through supplemental nutrition and nutrition education programs. The future of feeding diversity entails making space for diversity in food policy and nutrition instruction by drawing on the knowledge of cultural groups and creating flexibility for WIC-approved items. Feeding diversity also depends on an awareness of structural ethnocentrism, which can be as invisible as whiteness.

The author would like to thank Leilani Roughton, her staff, and clients at the New Arrivals Institute, Maurine Crouch, Kimberly Titlebaum, Dr. Art Murphy, Recipe for Success, University of North Carolina Greensboro, North Carolina Department of Health and Human Services, USDA SNAP-Ed, and the Wenner-Gren Foundation Dissertation Research Fellowship, which funded the research that provided comparative insights into Turkish culture. The author also thanks Dr. Mark Enfield for his thoughtful engagement with these ideas.

Bibliography

Douglas, Mary. 2003. *Purity and Danger: An Analysis of Concept of Pollution and Taboo.* London: Routledge.

DuPuis, E. Melanie. 2015. *Dangerous Digestion: The Politics of American Dietary Advice.* Berkeley: University of California Press.

Goffman, Erving. 1959. *The Presentation of Self in Everyday Life.* New York: Anchor.

Grotto, David, and Elisa Zied. 2010. "The Standard American Diet and Its Relationship to the Health Status of Americans." *Nutrition in Clinical Practice* 25 (6): 603–612.

Kremer-Sadlik, Tamar, Aliyah Morgenstern, Chloe Peters, Pauline Beaupoil, Stéphanie Caët, Camille Debras, and Marine le Mené. 2015. "Eating Fruits and Vegetables: An Ethnographic Study of American and French Family Dinners." *Appetite* 89: 84–92.

Lipsitz, George. (1998) 2006. *The Possessive Investment in Whiteness: How White People Profit from Identity Politics*, rev. ed. Philadelphia: Temple University Press.

Mintz, Sidney. W. 1986. *Sweetness and Power: The Place of Sugar in Modern History.* New York: Penguin Books.

Shklovsky, Viktor. 2016. *Viktor Shklovsky: A Reader.* Translated and edited by Alexandra Berlina. London: Bloomsbury.

Swagerty, Daniel L., Anne D. Walling, and Robert M. Klein. 2002. "Lactose Intolerance." *American Family Physician* 65, no. 9 (May 1, 2002): 1845–1850.

U.S. News and World Report. 2018. "U.S. News Best Diets: How We Ranked 40 Eating Plans." Accessed January 2018, http://health.usnews.com/wellness/food/articles/how-us-news-ranks-best-diets.

Wiedman, Dennis. 2012. "Native American Embodiment of the Chronicities of Modernity: Reservation Food, Diabetes, and the Metabolic Syndrome among the Kiowa, Comanche, and Apache." *Medical Anthropology Quarterly*, 26: 595–612. doi:10.1111/maq.12009.

CHAPTER 7

The Wu-Tang Clan and Cultural Resistance
Michael Blum

Over a gritty, up-tempo RZA beat, Ghostface Killah ends *Winter Warz* with "In Born Power, born physically, power speaking / The truth in the song be the pro-black teaching." While this bar is a tiny wave in the vast ocean of the group's catalog, it brings their politics to the surface. This is a rare a moment, because Clan members' politics remain buried in other facets of their lyrics.

The Wu-Tang Clan are not usually considered overtly political, or conscious, rappers—like Public Enemy. Instead, hip-hop scholarship focuses on other aspects of the group. Some scholarship omits the Clan or gives the group a cursory mention.[1] Other works cover the Clan's business model (Charnas 2010; George 1998). Several scholars identify a few elements of the group's lyrics but lack detailed analysis. The monographs on the Wu-Tang Clan use a chronological narrative to explain the group's rise and fall (Page 2014; Blanco 2011). As a whole, this scholarship fails to analyze the group's music as a site of resistance because they lack the contextualization and historicization necessary to fully understand their buried politics. Doing so reveals three facets of the Clan's sound—kung fu movies, Five Percent Nation of Islam theology, and street stories as sites of resistance to American racism, or as a well-hidden transcript, to paraphrase James C. Scott (1992).

When they burst onto the hip-hop scene in 1993, the Wu-Tang Clan featured nine members: RZA (Robert Diggs) the group's leader or abbot, GZA (Gary Grice), Ol' Dirty Bastard or ODB (Russell Jones), Method Man (Clifford Smith), Raekwon (Corey Woods), Ghostface Killah (Dennis Coles), Inspectah Deck (Jason Hunter), U-God (Lamont Hawkins), and Masta Killa (Elgin Turner). The Clan came together over several decades. Growing up, members met in school, by proximity, and sometimes through kin. The group's first album, *Enter the Wu-Tang*, put the Clan on the hip-hop map. With virtually no marketing, it sold more than two million copies. *The Source*'s Ghetto Communicator wrote that for fans of hardcore hip-hop, as opposed to pop rap like the recently popular Vanilla Ice and MC Hammer, "this is the hip-hop album you've been waiting for. Simply put: 'The Wu-Tang Clan ain't nuthin' to fuck with.'" *The Source* rated it four and one-half out of a possible five mics (Ghetto Communicator 1994). More than a decade later, critic Jared Dillon offered, "[T]here is no denying it is an essential and classic hip-hop album that, thanks to its originality and sheer talent, will go down in history as one of the key albums of the 1990s" (Dillon 2007). The combination of record sales and critical acclaim made the Clan major players in hip-hop.

Their next group album, *Wu-Tang Forever*, hit stores in 1997. It debuted at number one on both the "*Billboard* Top 200" and "R&B" charts. *Forever* sold more than four million copies and remains one of the top fifty selling hip-hop albums of all time. It also received favorable reviews. Neil Strauss of the *New York Times* reports that, with *Forever*, the group "retains its mantle as rap's standard bearers" (Strauss 1997). The album received a nomination for best rap album at the 1998 Grammy Awards. In 2000, they put out *The W*, the group's third album; and, shortly after, the group succumbed to internal squabbles. Members fought over creative differences and royalties. These problems were compounded by the overdose death of Ol' Dirty Bastard in 2004. While crew members continued to produce music and release group albums, they never achieved the success they experienced from 1993 to 1997.[2]

The Wu-Tang's success during the 1990s made them one of the most important groups of the decade. When they debuted, the Wu had a distinct sound, separating them from the competition. Gritty street tales, stories about events they lived or witnessed, serve as the foundation for the music. Wu-Tang's use of street tales serves several purposes. They demonstrate the Wu-Tang's authenticity by narrating the struggles they suffered growing up. This makes the group's lyrics real and therefore acceptable and believable to casual and skeptical hip-hop fans. Street stories also have a political purpose. Scholar and activist Angela Davis argues, "critical aesthetic representations of a social problem must be understood as constituting powerful social and political acts" (1998, 101). In this light, they can be read as illuminating the problems, including drugs and violence, faced by African Americans on Staten Island in attempts to bring about the social change needed to create a solution. They also provide a cinematic quality, which enlivens the listening experience.

Clan members' formative years created these street tales. All members were born within a six-year span ranging from 1966 to 1971. They, then, came of age during the late 1970s and early 1980s, a period of poverty and hardship for African American residents of New York City. Hip-hop scholar Tricia Rose argues, "Hip Hop's development in relationship to New York cultural politics in the 1970s is not unlike the relationship between other major cultural expressions and the broader social contexts within which they emerged. . . . [O]ther musically based cultural forms have developed at the junctures of major social transformation" (1994, 24–25). During the 1970s, major American cities experienced a transition. Information-based businesses replaced factories, which moved elsewhere for tax breaks and cheaper labor (ibid). The federal government cut funding for social services. In addition, corporate developers aggressively built luxury housing. As a result, working-class city dwellers were left with limited housing choices, few job opportunities, and minimal social services.

By 1975, New York City faced bankruptcy. It was saved by an agreement between the City and New York State, which obtained a federal loan in exchange for drastic cuts in city services and stringent repayment terms. As a result, 30 percent of the city's Hispanic population and 25 percent of the Black population lived in poverty (Rose 1994, 25–29). Historian Daniel Walkowitz observed that New York had become divided between white-collar workers and "an unemployed and underemployed service sector which is substantially Black and Hispanic" (1994, 29). Historian Jason Sokol describes New York City in the 1980s: "Streets were awash in crack cocaine and homelessness. The crime rate soared. The AIDS epidemic ravaged the city. New York was no longer the nation's urban gem" (Sokol 2014, 205).

The resulting gritty street tales offer insights into life on Staten Island. In "Cash Rules Everything Around Me (C.R.E.A.M.)," Raekwon (Wu-Tang 1993b) discusses his childhood:

> I grew up on the crime side, the *New York Times* side
> Staying alive was no jive
> Had second hands, moms bounced on old man
> So then we moved to Shaolin land
> A young youth, yo rockin' the gold tooth, 'Lo goose
> Only way I begin to G off was drug loot
> And let's start like this son, rollin' with this one
> And that one, pullin' out gats for fun
> But it was just a dream for the teen, who was a fiend
> Started smoking woolas at sixteen
> And running up in gates, and doing hits for high stakes
> Making my way on fire escapes

> No question I would speed, for cracks and weed
> The combination made my eyes bleed
> No question I would flow off, and try to get the dough all
> Sticking up white boys in ball courts.

Raekwon had a bleak childhood. Abandoned by his father, his family moved to Staten Island; and, thanks to his family's poverty, he was forced to wear secondhand clothing. To alleviate his poverty, he turned to the drug trade, robberies, and smoking *woolas* (marijuana cigars mixed with cocaine) at sixteen years old.

In "Tearz" (Wu-Tang 1993e), RZA narrates the story of Rakeem, the main character, and the murder of his brother:

> (Hey, Rakeem!) What? (Your little brother got shot!)
> I ran frantically, then I dropped down to his feet
> I saw the blood all over the hot concrete
> I picked him up then I held him by his head
> His eyes shut, that's when I knew he was . . .
> Aw man! How do I say goodbye?
> It's always the good ones that have to die
> Memories in the corner of my mind
> Flashbacks, I was laughing all the time
> I taught him all about the bees and birds.

RZA's lyrics paint a vivid picture of his brother's murder and the ensuing grief. He expresses an all-too-common sentiment among those who have had a relative murdered, a sadly common occurrence during the time.[3]

The Wu-Tang Clan did not originate street stories. This form of "reality rap" was introduced by Grand Master Flash and the Furious Five. In 1982, they released "The Message," the first commercially successful hip-hop song to discuss the struggle of African Americans in New York City. The first verse describes:

Broken glass everywhere
People pissing on the station
Y'know they just don't care
I can't take the smell
I can't take the noise
I got no money to move out
I guess I got no choice
Rats in the front room
Roaches in the back
Junkies in the alley with a baseball bat
I tries to get away but I couldn't get far
Cos a man with a truncheon re-possessed my car.

The rest of the song continues to address problems plaguing the Black community, including drug use, poor quality of education, and crime. The song, as hip-hop historian Dan Charnas notes, "reinforced the idea that rap could be serious, too, even meaningful" (2010, 88). This led Melle Mel (a member of the Furious Five) to record the anti-drug song, "White Lines (Don't Do It)," in 1983. Emerging around the same time, Run DMC, the first hip-hop superstars, adopted reality rap to broadcast life in Queens (Charnas 2010, 93–119). With the success of Run DMC, street tales became a staple of hip-hop.

Rapper and CEO Jay-Z once wrote, "Great rap should have all kinds of unresolved layers that you don't necessarily figure out the first time you listen to it" (2011, 54). Kung fu movies provide one of these layers. These movie samples are incorporated into the music, play a large part in the group's identity, and make a political statement. References to kung fu can be found in many songs. For example, "Bring the Ruckus" begins with a gravelly voice: "Shaolin shadowboxing and the Wu-Tang sword style / If what you say is true, the Shaolin and the Wu-Tang would be dangerous / Do you think your Wu-Tang sword can defeat me? En garde, I'll let you try my Wu-Tang style" (Wu-Tang 1993a). This quote comes from the 1983 kung fu movie, *Shaolin v. Wu-Tang*. In "Da Mystery of Chessboxin'," Masta Killa claims he is "moving on a nigga with the speed of a centipede" (Wu-Tang 1993c). The centipede is a martial arts style found in the movie *Five Deadly Venoms*.

The meaning of these kung fu movie samples is often misunderstood or goes unexplained. For example, Steve Juon in his review of *Enter the Wu-Tang* asserts, "There is a pure 'comedy' element to these films with their bad English translations and overdubbed dialog, but these films feature gifted athletes performing spectacular feats of strength and dexterity" (2001). Juon offers an Orientalized understanding of kung fu movies, which belittles the fact that they were not produced in English, does not analyze the plot, and fails to offer any ideas about the movies' larger meaning. This interpretation obscures their political implications.

During the 1970s, the Clan members' formative years, kung fu movies came to be understood differently in New York's Black community. Longtime hip-hop journalist Nelson George argues that kung fu movies served as a cultural response to Blaxploitation films, which relied on harmful Black stereotypes, such as the pimp and the gangster, to attract audiences. As an alternative, "Kung Fu [movies] provided a nonwhite, non-Western template for fighting [racial] superiority" (George 1998, 105). This reading is based on a common plot arc found in most kung fu movies: A marginalized character or group has an injustice done to them by a powerful ruler or group. To get revenge, the marginalized use their anger, determination, and martial arts skills to dethrone, kill, injure, or humiliate the powerful ruler or group. This postcolonial understanding was so common that in many Black households, a picture of Martin Luther King Jr. could often be found hanging near a poster of Bruce Lee, who George calls "a truly worthy nonwhite icon" (1998, 106).

As a youth, RZA understood kung fu movies as a metaphor for the plight of African Americans. He remembers,

> [W]hen I was a kid the only knowledge the media ever showed about Black history was about either slaves or pimps—*Roots*, *The Mack*, and that was basically it. So in a way films like *Thirty Six Chambers* reflected our experience and solidified it, drew people like me to our own history. And after that martial arts films became serious to me. (2009, 53)

In 1989, a kung fu movie cemented the group's identity. One day, RZA assembled a group of his friends, including Ghostface, ODB, and GZA, to smoke marijuana and watch *Eight Diagram Pole Fighter*, a kung fu movie in which a large family is betrayed by a military general. As a result, the family goes to war against the general. Eventually, six of the family's eight children are killed. Of the remaining two, one goes insane, and the other becomes a monk. About an hour into the movie, the viewers became quiet, and some started to cry. RZA explains, "You see this kind of thing happening in the 'hood every day. We were living in a place torn apart by wars . . . where the bonds you make are almost stronger than blood." As a result, the group "had to be called the Wu-Tang Clan. The name says we're Wu-Tang warriors, we're from Shaolin, and we're a Clan, which means family. The last part's crucial because it's a connection to something bigger than yourself, which is where the greatest strength always comes from" (2009, 57–58). Incorporating kung fu themes into their identity makes the struggle against American racism a foundation of the group.

One of the most misunderstood facets of the Wu-Tang is the influence of the Five Percent Nation of Islam (also called the Nation of Gods and Earths or the Five Percenters). The Five Percent Nation is an offshoot of the Nation of Islam (NOI). The group, founded in

1964 by Clarence Smith (also known as Clarence 13X), gained a following primarily among poor and working-class African Americans in northeastern cities, particularly New York.

Clarence 13X formed the Five Percent Nation to improve the lives of his followers. After working his way up the ranks at the Nation of Islam's Temple #7 in Harlem, he was expelled. The reason for his expulsion remains unclear. Some claim it resulted from Smith's gambling, drinking, infidelity, or conflicts with high-ranking mosque members, namely Louis Farrakhan and Malcolm X. While these reasons are difficult to substantiate, it is clear that Clarence 13X developed his own theology, which differed from the Nation of Islam's. The NOI taught that W. Fard Muhammad, the organization's founder, was God or Allah. Scholar Yusuf Nuruddin argues that 13X determined "Fard could not be God because the NOI lessons stated that the Original man or Black man was God and by appearance Fard was not Black. He reinterpreted the lessons and began to teach that it was not Fard, but the Black man collectively, who was God."[4]

The idea that the Black man is the original man and, therefore, God comes from the group's origin story. According to the teachings, the Black man is the maker, father of civilization, God of the Universe, and the original "inhabitor" of the planet (thefivepercentnation 2011b). One of these original men, a mad scientist named Yacub, broke from the group and created the white race (devils) who ruled the Black man for 6,000 years. After 6,000 years, Allah will destroy the devils to prove that he is all-powerful (thefivepercentnation 2011a).

To readers who are not members, their origin story may seem confusing. It should not be interpreted literally. Instead, it is better understood as an allegory about the experience of African Americans in the United States. Not all whites are devils. The devil is the racism that oppresses nonwhites in the United States. To combat racism, Allah made Black men God, thereby giving them the power to bring the devil's 6,000-year reign to an end. Making Black men Gods provides a sense of empowerment that combats the damaging psychological effects of racism and encourages Black men to break the structural barriers that limited Black economic and physical mobility. After all, Gods can do anything.

13X named the group after a foundational teaching found in "Lost and Found Muslim Lesson No. 2" (thefivepercentnation 2011a), an important NOI theological text. The Lesson explains that the world is divided into three groups. Eighty-five percent of the earth's population are uncivilized, do not follow the correct God, and are easily led in the wrong direction. Ten percent of the population make slaves of the poor by teaching them to follow a false god. The last five percent are the wise who understand that the Black man is God and teach freedom, justice, and equality to all humans (Allah 2009, 122). The mission of the Five Percent is to teach the eighty-five percent to follow the Five Percent Nation.

Since the Black man himself is God, he is free to interpret the world as he sees fit. To do so, Five Percent members memorize a series of NOI religious texts collectively called the "120 Lessons." They are composed of five documents: "Student Enrollment 1–10," "Lost Found Muslim Lesson No. 1," "Lost Found Muslim Lesson No. 2," "Actual Facts," and "Solar Facts." The first three documents are written in a question-and-answer format to teach new followers the group's dogma. In combination, these documents provide a basic education in the group's theology and interpretation of race relations, science, geography, and philosophy. They provide the often-undereducated members with elements of a formal education.

In addition, Five Percenters study the Supreme Mathematics and Supreme Alphabet, a pair of systems created by Clarence 13X in which a number or letter is substituted for a word, phrase, or concept. The world is then interpreted through numerology. The Supreme Mathematics is as follows:

1) Knowledge
2) Wisdom
3) Understanding
4) Culture or Freedom
5) Power
6) Equality
7) God
8) Build or Destroy
9) Born
0) Cipher

(Allah 2009, 118–9)

When these numbers appear to Five Percenters, they provide guidance. For example, if a follower won eight dollars, he might give to a charity that helps build homes for the poor. The number eight means "build" and serves as a sign for the money's purpose. RZA explains, "Mathematics is what we live. And the numerology side of it makes you aware of the connections between everything" (RZA 2009, 41). The Supreme Alphabet offers a similar means of interpretation through letters.

More generally, the 120 Lessons reinforce the Five Percent Nation's nine tenets. They are:

> Black people are the original inhabitants of the planet.
>
> Black people are the mothers and fathers of civilization.
>
> The Supreme Mathematics provides understanding of man's relationship to the universe.
>
> Islam is a way of life, not just a religion.
>
> Education should be used to make Black people self-sufficient.
>
> All followers should teach others.

> The Black man is God and his proper name is Allah.
>
> Children are the future and should be loved, protected, and educated.
>
> A unified Black family is the key to building the nation.

These tenets offer a self-help plan similar to the one espoused by Elijah Muhammad and Malcolm X during the early 1960s. The plan is pragmatic and well within the tradition of Black nationalist thought. It promotes conservative ideas such as education, self-sufficiency, and a strong family, which serve to create a strong and independent Black community. It also includes several radical ideas. The first two tenets contradict the feeling that African Americans belong at the bottom of society by teaching that they are the originators of civilization and should therefore hold themselves in high esteem. The promotion of Islam challenges the idea that the United States is a Christian nation. Instead, Black nationalists commonly cast Christianity as the slaveholder's religion and Islam as its revolutionary antithesis. Finally, rather than creating loyal citizens, it calls for an education that will teach Black people to free themselves from dependence on whites. In combination, they offer a means to combat racism.

The Five Percent Nation's teachings resonated with young Black men. Ethnomusicologist Christina Zanfagna (2015, 74) observes:

> For young Black men, Clarence 13X's teachings provided the structure in the midst of the chaos associated with everyday life on the streets. Furthermore, young Five Percenters are renowned for their tremendous oral skills, gained through drilling lessons and through street preaching. This skill set meshed well with the verbal dexterity and performative charisma required in Hip Hop MCing.

This proved to be true for a young Robert Diggs. RZA recalls that in 1981, his cousin GZA introduced him to the Five Percent Nation's theology. "That snapped a revelation inside my head. That was the first time I heard something that made sense externally and internally. Being in poverty and one of the oppressed people in America, you know you are limited, but feel like you shouldn't be" (RZA 2009, 41). A year later, at age twelve, RZA committed all 120 Lessons to memory. He then began teaching others, including his cousin ODB. After hearing his teenage peers recite some of the teachings, Five Percent Nation historian Wakeel Allah (2009, 17) recalls,

> [T]o a young impressionable mind that was seeking the truth and knowledge of Black History it was captivating. Especially, when you seen [sic] one of your peers embrace this teaching and then blossom to become very cool with a newly loaded vocabulary that made them appear smarter than the school teachers.

For Allah, these teachings challenged the idea that young Black men lacked the desire to succeed. Instead, "the message we received was be all that you can be . . . you are GOD" (Allah 2009, 17). The teachings injected a sense of pride into the difficult lives of poor Black men.

The Five Percent Nation's theology is common in Wu-Tang lyrics. "Wu Revolution," the first track on *Wu-Tang Forever*, features Clan affiliate Papa Wu reciting the Five Percent Nation's origin story (Wu-Tang 1997). In "Protect Ya Neck" (Wu-Tang 1993d), Raekwon explains that he has "thoughts that bomb shit like math!" This line references the power of the Supreme Mathematics to change listeners' worldview. During a skit at the beginning of "Wu-Tang: 7th Chamber" (Wu-Tang 1993f), Ghostface Killah announces that he arrives to get his "culture cipher." Here he is referring to the Supreme

Mathematics, where four means culture and zero means cipher. In the skit, Ghostface enters the room to get his forty-ounce beer.

Wu-Tang is not the first crew to be influenced by the Five Percent Nation. As music scholar Felicia Miyakawa (2005) demonstrates, throughout hip-hop's history, rappers, including Pete Rock and C. L. Smooth, Rakim, and Big Daddy Kane, have incorporated Five Percent teachings into their lyrics. She argues these "Five Percent MCs bring their doctrine to the public's ears by presenting themselves as authoritative teachers; offering personal testimonials; and quoting, paraphrasing, and interpreting Five Percenter lessons and other teachings . . . to both reach out to the 'uncivilized' masses and share communal messages with listeners already familiar." [5]

Overall, the Wu-Tang Clan's music can be understood as a site of resistance against American racism. Through contextualizing and historicizing three important facets of the group's lyrics, fans can understand how they are used to fight racism. Given the Wu-Tang Clan's popularity and continuing influence, these are powerful forces in this struggle. In terms of hip-hop scholarship, this analysis provides a different reading of the group's lyrics, demonstrates another reason for the group's success, and extends the chronological scope of the "golden age of rap nationalism" as put forth by scholar Charise Cheney. [6]

The author would like to thank Brandon Jet for his helpful comments.

Notes

1. These books fall into two categories. The first provides a cultural analysis of hip-hop, which includes topics such as politics, misogyny, and the genre's relation to postmodernism: Tricia Rose, *Black Noise: Rap Music and Black Culture in Contemporary America*; Russell A. Potter, *Spectacular Vernaculars: Hip-Hop and the Politics of Postmodernism*; Jeffrey O. G. Ogbar, *Hip-Hop Revolution: The Culture and Politics of Rap*; Tricia Rose, *The Hip Hop Wars: What We Talk About When We Talk About Hip Hop—and Why It Matters*. The others give a cursory mention: Jeff Chang, *Can't Stop Won't Stop: A History of the Hip-Hop Generation*; S. Craig Watkins, *Hip Hop Matters: Politics, Pop Culture, and the Struggle for the Soul of a Movement*; William Eric Perkins, ed., *Droppin' Science: Critical Essays on Rap Music and Hip Hop Culture*; Murray Forman and Mark Anthony Neal, eds., *That's the Joint!: The Hip-Hop Studies Reader*.

2. Because this is a conference paper, I have limited its scope to focus on *Enter the Wu-Tang (36 Chambers)* and *Wu-Tang Forever*. Additional analysis of the solo albums released during this period would expand the paper well beyond the page limit.

3. The frequent use of street stories is part of the Clan's authenticity. Hip-hop scholar Jeffery O. G. Ogbar argues that authenticity is hip-hop's "essential character." However, authenticity is a "nebulous nation," which is created, "negotiated, interrogated, and articulated in a world where gendered and racialized stereotypes are pervasive" (Ogbar 2007, 1, 5) For the Wu-Tang Clan, their listening experience provides authenticity. It combines well-established means of proving realness, namely street stories and slang, with previously unseen facets, kung fu movies, and RZA's production to provide their own take on authenticity.

4. Yusuf Nuruddin, "The Five Percenters: A Teenage Nation of Gods and Earths," in Wakeel Allah, *In the Name of Allah: A History of Clarence 13X and the Five Percenters* (2009, vol. 1, 88). Allah also points out that while his place of birth remains unknown, many who met him claimed he may have been from the Middle East or North Africa because of his skin tone and other physical features (23–28).

5. The Wu-Tang's incorporation of the Five Percent nation pushes the study of religion in hip-hop. Beyond the first wave, which debated the relationship between pious religion and profane hip-hop, the Clan pushes scholars to examine the multiple functions of religion in their lyrics. It is political, literary, and an important part of the group's identity and authenticity (Monica Miller, Anthony Pinn, and Bernard "Bun B" Freeman, eds., *Religion in Hip Hop: Mapping the New Terrain in the US*).

6. The Wu-Tang Clan's continued promotion of the Five Percent Nation extends the chronology of Charise Cheney. She claims that "gangsta rap ended the golden age of rap nationalism." However, the Wu-Tang preached Black Nationalism vis-a-via Five Percent Nation theology, at least, through 1997. The Wu-Tang Clan's music was popular at the same time as several seminal gangsta rap albums, including Dr. Dre's *The Chronic*, Snoop Doggy Dogg's *Doggystyle*, and Ice Cube's *Lethal Injection*, demonstrating that rap nationalism and gangsta rap existed simultaneously (Charise Cheney, *Brothers Gonna Work It Out: Sexual Politics in the Golden Age of Rap Nationalism*, p. 150).

Bibliography

Allah, Wakeel. 2009. *In the Name of Allah: A History of Clarence 13X and the Five Percenters.* Atlanta: A-Team Publishing.

Blanco, Alvin. 2011. *The Wu Tang Clan and RZA: A Trip Through Hip Hop's 36 Chambers.* Santa Barbara, CA: Praeger.

Chang, Jeff. 2005. *Can't Stop Won't Stop: A History of the Hip-Hop Generation.* New York: Picador.

Charnas, Dan. 2010. *The Big Payback: The History of the Business of Hip-Hop.* New York: New American Library.

Cheney, Charise, 2005. *Brothers Gonna Work It Out: Sexual Politics in the Golden Age of Rap Nationalism.* New York: New York University Press.

Davis, Angela Y. 1999. *Blues Legacies and Black Feminism: Gertrude "Ma" Rainey, Bessie Smith and Billie Holiday.* New York: Vintage.

Dillon, Jared. 2007 "Enter the Wu Tang (36 Chambers)," *Sputnikmusic.com*, February 13, 2007.

Forman, Murray, and Mark Anthony Neal, eds. 2004. *That's the Joint!: The Hip-Hop Studies Reader.* New York: Routledge.

George, Nelson. 1998. *Hip-Hop America.* New York: Penguin.

Ghetto Communicator. 1994. "Enter The Wu-Tang 36 Chambers." *The Source*, February 1994.

Ghostface Killah [Dennis Coles]. 1996. "Winter Warz." On *Ironman*, featuring Cappadonna, U-God, and Masta Killa. Epic/Sony Records.

Grand Master Flash and the Furious Five. 1982. "The Message." On *The Message.* Sugar Hill Records.

Jay-Z [Shawn Carter]. 2010. *Decoded.* New York: Spiegel and Grau.

Juon, Steve. 2001. "Enter the Wu-Tang (36 Chambers)." Rapreviews.com, April 17, 2001.

Mel, Melle. 1983. "White Lines (Don't Do It)." Single. Sugar Hill Records.

Miller, Monica R., Anthony B. Pinn, and Bernard "Bun B" Freeman, eds. 2015. *Religion In Hip Hop: Mapping the New Terrain in the US.* New York: Bloomsbury Academic.

Miyakawa, Felicia M. 2005. *Five Percenter Rap: God Hop's Music, Message, and Black Muslim Mission*. Bloomington: Indiana University Press.

Ogbar, Jeffrey O. G. 2007. *Hip-Hop Revolution: The Culture and Politics of Rap*. Lawrence: University of Kansas Press.

Page, Alan C. 2014. *Enter the Wu Tang: How Nine Men Changed Hip-Hop Forever*. New York: Lone Gunman Media.

Perkins, William Eric, ed. 1996. *Droppin' Science: Critical Essays on Rap Music and Hip Hop Culture*. Philadelphia: Temple University Press.

Potter, Russell A. 1995. *Spectacular Vernaculars: Hip-Hop and the Politics of Postmodernism*. Albany: State University of New York Press.

Rose, Tricia. 1994. *Black Noise: Rap Music and Black Culture in Contemporary America*. Middletown, CT: Wesleyan University Press.

Rose, Tricia. 2008. *The Hip Hop Wars: What We Talk about When We Talk About Hip Hop—and Why It Matters*. New York: BasicCivitas.

RZA [Robert Diggs] and Chris Norris. 2009. *The Tao of Wu*. New York: Riverhead.

Scott, James C. 1992. *Domination and the Arts of Resistance: Hidden Transcripts*, new ed. New Haven: Yale University Press.

Sokol, Jason. 2014. *All Eyes Are Upon Us: Race and Politics from Boston to Brooklyn*. New York: Basic Books.

Strauss, Neil. 1997. "Strains of Violin in Slick, Smooth Rap." *New York Times*, June 10, 1997.

thefivepercentnation. 2011a. "Lost Found Muslim Lesson No. 2 (1–40)." *thefivepercentnation* (blog), May 1, 2011. http://thefivepercentnation. wordpress.com/2011/05/01/lost-found-muslim-lesson-no-2-1-40.

thefivepercentnation. 2011b. "Student Enrollment (1–10)" *thefivepercentnation* (blog), March 15, 2011. https://thefivepercentnation.wordpress. com/2011/03/15/student-enrollment-1-10.

Walkowitz, Daniel. 1994. "New York: A Tale of Two Cities." In Tricia Rose, *Black Noise: Rap Music and Black Culture in Contemporary America*, 29. Hanover, NH: Wesleyan University Press.

Watkins, S. Craig. 2005. *Hip-Hop Matters: Politics, Pop Culture, and the Struggle for the Soul of a Movement*. Boston: Beacon Press.

Wu-Tang Clan. 1993a. "Bring the Ruckus." On *Enter the Wu-Tang (36 Chambers)*. Loud/MCA Records.

———. 1993b. "Cash Rules Everything Around Me (C.R.E.A.M.)." On *Enter the Wu-Tang (36 Chambers)*. Loud/MCA Records.

———. 1993c. "Da Mystery of Chessboxin'." On *Enter the Wu-Tang (36 Chambers)*. Loud/MCA Records.

———. 1993d. "Protect Ya Neck." On *Enter the Wu-Tang (36 Chambers)*. Loud/MCA Records.

———. 1993e. "Tearz." On *Enter the Wu-Tang (36 Chambers)*. Loud/MCA Records.

———. 1993f. "Wu Tang: 7th Chamber." On *Enter the Wu-Tang (36 Chambers)*. Loud/MCA Records.

———. 1997. "Wu Revolution." On *Wu-Tang Forever*. Loud/MCA Records.

Zanfagna, Christina. 2015. "Hip-Hop and Religion: From the Mosque to the Church." In *The Cambridge Companion to Hip-Hop*, edited by Justin A. Williams. Cambridge: Cambridge University Press.

About the Contributors

MICHAEL BLUM teaches English and history at NEXT High School in Greenville, South Carolina. His research focuses on the Civil Rights Movement and, more recently, the Wu-Tang Clan. He received a PhD in African American History from the University of Memphis in 2014.

YEJU "CHLOE" CHOI works as a Training Specialist at a multinational corporation. She received her MS in Conflict Management and PhD in International Conflict Management from Kennesaw State University. Her research interests include the role of leadership in cross-cultural conflict and communication. She has published five refereed journal articles and presented eleven refereed conference presentations at international, national, and regional-level conferences. She is also a Registered Neutral in the State of Georgia and served as a Managing Editor and Resources Editor for the *Journal of Peacebuilding and Development* and as an Editorial Assistant to *Conflict Resolution Quarterly*.

KEZIA DARKWAH is a graduate of the PhD program in International Conflict Management in the School of Conflict Management, Peacebuilding, and Development at Kennesaw State University. She provides consulting services in immigrant and host communities.

DANIEL W. INGERSOLL JR. is Professor Emeritus of Anthropology, St. Mary's College of Maryland. His interests include historical archaeology, experimental archaeology, material culture analysis, symbolism, Rapa Nui landscapes, and agricultural pesticides.

KATHLEEN INGERSOLL's research interests include historic landscapes and gardens, the intersection of eco-tourism and historic preservation, and museum studies. She holds a PhD from the University of York, UK.

CHRISTINE KOVIC is Professor of Anthropology and Cross-Cultural Studies at the University of Houston–Clear Lake. She has conducted research in the field of human rights for the past 25 years. Her current research addresses the intersection of human rights, health, and immigration, with emphasis on Central American migrants crossing Mexico in the journey north and on the human rights and organizing efforts of Latinxs in the United States.

BRANDON D. LUNDY is a Professor of Anthropology in the Geography and Anthropology Department and the Associate Director for the PhD Program in International Conflict Management in the School of Conflict Management, Peacebuilding, and Development at Kennesaw State University.

AYLA SAMLI is a researcher and writer who seeks out the intersections of culture and creativity, humanism, and representation. She has a PhD in cultural anthropology from Rice University and an MFA in creative writing from Queen's University of Charlotte. She lives and teaches in North Carolina.

MARJORIE M. SNIPES is Professor of Anthropology at University of West Georgia. Her research focuses on religion, identity, and culture change in the Andes of Northwestern Argentina and with religious groups in the United States.

www.ingramcontent.com/pod-product-compliance
Lightning Source LLC
Chambersburg PA
CBHW031445280326
41927CB00037B/359